A Concise Guide to
Education
Studies

EDUCATION
STUDIES

A Concise Guide to

Education Studies

EDUCATION STUDIES

DUNCAN HINDMARCH, FIONA HALL, LYNN MACHIN & SANDRA MURRAY

First published in 2017 by Critical Publishing Ltd

British Library Cataloguing in Publication Data
A CIP record for this book is available from the British Library

ISBN: 978-1-911106-80-7

This book is also available in the following e-book formats:

MOBI ISBN: 978-1-911106-81-4
EPUB ISBN: 978-1-911106-82-1
Adobe e-book ISBN: 978-1-911106-83-8

Text design by Greensplash Limited
Cover design by Out of House Limited
Project management by Out of House Publishing
Printed and bound in Great Britain by TJ International, Padstow, Cornwall

Critical Publishing
3 Connaught Road
St Albans
AL3 5RX

www.criticalpublishing.com

MIX
Paper from
responsible sources
FSC® C013056

To order please go to our website www.criticalpublishing.com or contact our distributor, NBN International, 10 Thornbury Road, Plymouth PL6 7PP, telephone 01752 202301 or email orders@nbninternational.com.

Contents

Meet the authors

Duncan Hindmarch is a course leader and senior lecturer within the School of Life Sciences and Education at Staffordshire University. With a background in teaching English for Speakers of Other Languages (ESOL), he has 20 years of teaching experience. Duncan is a Senior Fellow of the Higher Education Academy and Society for Education and Training and has led development and implementation of ESOL, initial teacher education (ITE) and other education programmes. He has co-authored a series of books for further education (FE) teachers and also a book entitled *Supporting Primary Teaching and Learning*, all published by Critical Publishing.

Fiona Hall is a course leader within the School of Life Sciences and Education at Staffordshire University. She has more than 20 years' of experience of working within primary, FE and higher education (HE). She has also been involved in teacher training in FE undertaking teacher observations. Her current research interests are situated in the exploration of teaching assistant practice in schools. Fiona has co-authored *Supporting Primary Teaching and Learning* and *A Concise Guide to the Level 3 Award in Education and Training*.

Lynn Machin is an award leader, senior lecturer, PhD admissions tutor and a supervisor for students undertaking doctoral studies within the School of Life Sciences and Education at Staffordshire University. Lynn has more than 25 years of experience working within FE and HE. Many of these years have been spent designing and delivering initial teacher education for trainees who work, or want to work, in the FE sector. Over the past few years her skills and knowledge in this area have been used to design and deliver programmes in Sub-Saharan Africa and also in Asia. Her current research interests include an exploration of how students can develop their capacities to learn and grow as self-directed and autonomous learners. Lynn has co-authored a series of books for teachers within FE. She has also written chapters in several other books including *Supporting Primary Teaching and Learning* and *Post Compulsory Teacher Educators: Connecting Professionals*.

Sandra Murray is a lecturer within the School of Life Sciences and Education at Staffordshire University. Having taught for many years in an FE college, she has a wide range of experience supporting and teaching teachers in the FE sector and has been teaching on initial teacher education programmes since 2006. Her particular research interest is inspirational and outstanding teaching. She has co-authored several books for teachers within FE.

Chapter links to the QAA Subject Benchmark Statements: Education Studies

Knowledge and understanding
On graduating with an honours degree in education studies, students should demonstrate a critical understanding of:

Benchmark statement	Chapter coverage
The underlying values, theories and concepts relevant to education.	2, 3, 4, 5, 6, 7
The diversity of learners and the complexities of the education process.	4, 5, 6, 7
The complexity of the interaction between learning and local and global contexts, and the extent to which participants (including learners and teachers) can influence the learning process.	3, 8
The societal and organisational structures and purposes of educational systems, and the possible implications for learners and the learning process.	2, 5, 6

Application
On graduating with an honours degree in education studies, students should be able to demonstrate the ability to:

Benchmark statement	Chapter coverage
Analyse educational concepts, theories and issues of policy in a systematic way.	2, 3, 4, 7, 8
Identify and reflect on potential connections and discontinuities between each of the aspects of subject knowledge and their application in educational policies and contexts.	4
Accommodate new principles and understandings.	3, 7, 10
Select a range of relevant primary and secondary sources, including theoretical and research-based evidence, to extend their knowledge and understanding.	9
Use a range of evidence to formulate appropriate and justified ways forward and potential changes in practice.	2, 6, 9, 10

Reflection
On graduating with an honours degree in education studies, students should be able to demonstrate:

Benchmark statement	Chapter coverage
The ability to reflect on their own and others' value systems.	1, 2, 5
The ability to use their knowledge and understanding critically to locate and justify a personal position in relation to the subject.	1, 3
An understanding of the significance and limitations of theory and research.	1, 3, 8, 9

Transferable skills On graduating with an honours degree in education studies, students should be able to:	
Benchmark statement	**Chapter coverage**
Communication and presentation Organise and articulate opinions and arguments in speech and writing using relevant specialist vocabulary.	1
Technology Use technology effectively to enhance critical and reflective study.	10
Application of numerical skills Collect and apply numerical data, as appropriate. Present data in a variety of formats including graphical and tabular. Analyse and interpret both qualitative and quantitative data.	9
Working with others Collaborate and plan as part of a team, to carry out roles allocated by the team and take the lead where appropriate, and to fulfil agreed responsibilities.	6
Improving own learning and performance Articulate their own approaches to learning and organise an effective work pattern including working to deadlines.	9
Analytical and problem-solving skills Process and synthesise empirical and theoretical data, to create new syntheses and to present and justify a chosen position having drawn on relevant theoretical perspectives.	1, 2

QAA (2015) *Subject Benchmark Statement: Education Studies.* [Online]. Retrieved from www.qaa.ac.uk/en/Publications/Documents/SBS-education-studies-15.pdf (accessed 23 April 2017).

Introduction

THE AIM OF THIS BOOK

The aim of this book is to support you in developing your knowledge of contemporary issues within the UK education sector and your understanding of how these impact on learners and professionals. It also supports your development as a critically reflective academic thinker. It achieves these aims by providing:

o   an outline of key current education policy developments and their impact on teachers, learners and learning;

o   up-to-date overviews of the evidence and ideologies that inform key debates within the education sector;

o   a chapter that is specifically focused on the development of critical thinking skills;

o   activities and questions within each chapter;

o   recommendations for further reading at the end of each chapter.

WHO SHOULD READ THIS BOOK?

This book is intended to support you in your studies including:

o   a BA education studies undergraduate course, with or without QTS;

o   as an initial starting point prior to commencing MA-level education studies;

o   teacher training;

o   self-study for professional development.

CONTENT AND STRUCTURE

Chapter structure

All of the chapters follow a similar structure:

o   a visual map displays the structure of the chapter and highlights the topics that are discussed;

o   a brief introduction;

o   subject expertise and professional links providing coverage of the QAA *Subject Benchmark Statements: Education Studies*;

- chapter objectives;

- activities and questions to develop critical thinking;

- a summary of key points;

- 'check your understanding' questions at the end of the chapter;

- recommendations for further reading;

- references.

Chapter content

The book has ten chapters, each of which cover a different theme or topic.

Chapter 1 Thinking critically to become a high achieving practitioner

This chapter examines principles of critical thinking, reading and writing. It also discusses how to use evidence effectively to make critically informed and evidence-based reflections and decisions.

Chapter 2 The historical context of English education (1988–the present)

This chapter outlines some of the education policies that have had an impact on teachers, learners and learning. It covers topics relating to the national curriculum, raising the school leaving age, regulatory requirements and competition in a global environment.

Chapter 3 Current approaches to teaching, learning and assessment

This chapter gives an overview of current policy direction and underpinning ideology in framing academic and vocational learning strategies. It highlights the focus on the growing importance placed on maths and English/literacy within the curriculum as well as the ideologies and policies that are driving this.

Chapter 4 Perspectives on safeguarding and behaviour strategies

This chapter charts the development of safeguarding policies, the promotion of British values and anti-radicalisation. Additionally, it examines issues relating to behaviour management.

Chapter 5 Inclusion, equality and special educational needs

This chapter presents key terms and historical perspectives regarding the effectiveness of education strategies to promote inclusion, equality and SEND.

Chapter 6 Leadership, management, teamwork and quality

This chapter considers accountability, quality assurance and improvement measures in education including an oversight of Ofsted and independent school equivalents. It also considers the shaping of education structures relating to academisation, free schools, maintained and independent schools, FE colleges and private training providers. Finally, it examines theories of leadership and characteristics of teams.

Chapter 7 Adult, family and community education

This chapter shapes an outline of some of the policies and practices to promote lifelong learning outside the school system. These include, for example, community and family education, education for the elderly and prison and offender education.

Chapter 8 Comparative education: learning from other countries

This chapter outlines how national education systems are measured globally, considering benefits of comparative education (CE) as well as criticisms of its methodologies and how findings are interpreted. It then evaluates how CE influences UK education policy.

Chapter 9 Making a difference: practitioner-led research

This chapter reviews some of the purposes, approaches and validity of practitioner-led research. It explores the role of research within education, focusing on the process of practitioner-led research as a way of improving professional practice.

Chapter 10 Looking to the future: education technology

This chapter evaluates policy drivers relating to the development of technology within education and examines some of the impact that the use of technology can have on learners and the teaching and learning environment.

There is a glossary at the end of the book that provides a brief explanation of key terms used within the chapters.

Enjoy reading!

Thinking critically to become a high achieving practitioner

Sourcing and analysing information

Principles of critical thinking

The importance of critical thinking

Forming and using judgements

Thinking critically to become a high achieving practitioner

Limitations of critical thinking

Critical thinking and professional practice

Teaching critical thinking

Critical thinking and teacher standards

INTRODUCTION

Critical thinking (CT) is a key component of your personal, professional and academic development. It features prominently in the some of the UK's teachers' standards as well as being explicitly highlighted in the QAA's definition of undergraduate education studies courses:

> *Essentially, education studies is concerned with understanding how people develop and learn throughout their lives, and the nature of knowledge and critical engagement with ways of knowing and understanding.*

> (QAA, 2015, p 6)

Moon (2008), however, highlights numerous contrasting definitions of the term within academia with Moore (2013) finding seven differing interpretations within one HE institution alone. Furthermore, Higgins (2014) questions its importance in relation to other thinking skills such as creativity, as well as how it should be developed and applied. This chapter outlines key definitions, approaches and limitations of CT while also highlighting expectations within professional and academic standards. Your ability to develop a consistently critical stance towards information has a major influence on your professional career and personal journey through life.

SUBJECT EXPERTISE LINKS

Developing critical thinking (CT) is a central component of higher education studies.

> *Students have opportunities to develop their critical capabilities through the selection, analysis and synthesis of relevant perspectives, and to be able to justify different positions on educational matters.*

> (QAA, 2015, p 6)

This chapter helps you work towards the following QAA (2015) *Subject Benchmark Statement: Education Studies* standards.

Reflection

○ The ability to reflect on their own and others' value systems.

○ The ability to use their knowledge and understanding critically to locate and justify a personal position in relation to the subject.

○ An understanding of the significance and limitations of theory and research.

Communication and presentation

○ Organise and articulate opinions and arguments in speech and writing using relevant specialist vocabulary.

Transferable skills

○ Process and synthesise empirical and theoretical data, to create new syntheses and to present and justify a chosen position having drawn on relevant theoretical perspectives.

OBJECTIVES

This chapter introduces underpinning principles of CT, outlining differing conceptual viewpoints as well as developing your understanding of how and why it should be applied in academic and professional practice.

This chapter develops your understanding of CT in terms of:

○ principles;

○ development strategies;

○ its role in academic and professional practice;

○ limitations.

PRINCIPLES OF CRITICAL THINKING

The importance of critical thinking

Recently, phrases such as 'post-truth' and 'fake news' have risen to prominence following the Brexit and American presidential campaigns, where demonstrably false claims were repeatedly made for electoral gain (Peters, 2017). When challenged over these, responses related to having rights to voice differing opinions, oxymoronically defined as 'alternative facts', or representing the true voice of the people over educated elites. Thus Michael Gove dismissed the evaluations of numerous renowned authorities by declaring: *I think the people of this country have had enough of experts* (Sky News, 2016), a casual dismissal of evidence and expertise that raises the question of what value he saw in his previous role as Secretary of State for Education. Indeed, reflecting on the rising popularity of anti-intellectual culture, Hoffman (2016) cites several surveys demonstrating declining public awareness of key scientific issues as evidence of a breakdown in informed public policy discourse. Peters argues in-depth research and analysis therefore face direct threats from the speed and reach of social media:

> It's not so much that facts are futile, it's just that they take a while to collect and marshal into a knock-down argument. By the time the facts are gathered the media moment has passed, the headline has been grabbed, and the lie can be modified, apologised for or replaced by another.

(Peters, 2017, p 3)

Regardless of the extent to which current affairs genuinely represent a new paradigm, such events illustrate the importance of CT as a necessary means of examining, substantiating or challenging the basis of decisions that affect our everyday lives. Challenging lies, ignorant, ill-informed or maliciously twisted information is not being part of an 'intellectual elite', but a crucial part of being an academic (Hoffman, 2016), professional employee and constructive citizen within society (Facione, 2015). It is important to remember that the point of researching evidence should not be to unwaveringly support your personal viewpoints or predispositions, but to challenge, and in all likelihood change, your own opinions and understandings. By being better informed, you can unearth your own prejudices and misunderstandings, thereby improving your own comprehension of, and contribution to, the world.

Moore's (2013) study of literature and academics' understandings of CT found a consensus regarding its importance, but no such agreement regarding its definition or implementation approaches. There is even dispute regarding whether it should be considered an unchanging set of principles, context-dependent or limited within subject areas. Regarding the first view of CT, the American Philosophical Association formed an expert consensus that has been subsequently frequently cited:

> *The ideal critical thinker is habitually inquisitive, well-informed, trustful of reason, open-minded, flexible, fair-minded in evaluation, honest in facing personal biases, prudent in making judgments, willing to reconsider, clear about issues, orderly in complex matters, diligent in seeking relevant information, reasonable in the selection of criteria, focused in inquiry, and persistent in seeking results which are as precise as the subject and the circumstances of inquiry permit.*
> (American Philosophical Association, 1990, cited in Facione, 2015, p 27)

Although recognising differing approaches to CT, Elder and Paul (2010) take the idea of defining underlying principles further, developing *Universal Intellectual Standards*: clarity, accuracy, precision, relevance, depth, breadth, logic, significance and fairness, which underpin thought processes and intellectual traits or virtues. Vaughn (2015) further advocates the value of a systematic, process-based approach with distinct procedures and methods, although Mulnix (2012) warns that this alone is insufficient, urging repeated practice to embed and continually develop CT ability. Countering the above viewpoints, Willingham's research (2008) emphasises the importance of in-depth subject knowledge as a precursor to CT, arguing that limited outcomes of generic skills development programmes evidence his view that CT skills are discipline specific and lack transferability. Clinchy (1993, cited in Moore, 2013), considers that CT depends on the context that it will be applied in, requiring either *separate knowing*, a dispassionate approach to evaluating evidence, or *connected knowing*, where the focus is on insight from individuals and groups. Barnett (1997, cited in Moore, 2013) also favours differing modes depending on its purpose: subject competence, practical knowledge, political engagement and strategic thinking.

While there is disagreement regarding whether and how CT should be defined and taught, there are some common aspects that can help us to identify CT and how we may apply it to our personal and professional lives.

Sourcing and analysing information

○   Having a clear focus to your investigation.

○   Acquiring relevant information from multiple sources.

○   Systematically organising evidence.

○   Identifying key themes and inferring meaningful connections.

○   Comparing and contrasting differing evidence.

○   Evaluating the quality of evidence.

○   Reflecting on and potentially amending your original focus.

Forming and using judgements

○   Making a fair, transparent and reflexive judgement based on the available evidence.

○   Transparently acknowledging personal influences and interests that may influence your judgement as well as how you have sought to overcome/limit this impact.

○   Clearly articulating your judgement, its scope and limitations.

○   Acting on your judgement.

○   Developing or changing your judgement when new evidence emerges.

Mulnix (2012) and Moore (2013) additionally found that some academics view a key purpose of CT being to challenge established hierarchies. However, Mulnix (2012) demonstrates that such an approach contradicts the underlying purpose of CT being to seek out truths as far as possible. Indeed, a key purpose of seeking evidence should not be to reaffirm your existing understandings (and prejudices), but to challenge and even change them.

Sourcing and analysing information

Initiating critical thought processes requires identifying key questions to answer, although these may develop based on new understanding throughout your investigation. This enables discernment of relevant information against interesting but irrelevant information. A critical thinker does not accept without evaluation the first piece of information they find. Information literacy is therefore vital; being able to identify and draw from a range of authoritative sources while retaining a keen and sceptical eye for underlying biases and agendas in any source (Facione, 2015). This means not just accepting a single point of view, however authoritative, but trying to find different sources of information on the chosen subject. All sources have some form of underlying bias, which to a greater or lesser extent may influence its findings and credibility. Furthermore, your personal experiences and viewpoints affect how you select, evaluate and interpret what you read. An ability to think reflexively to understand these influences can help you challenge your own assumptions and prejudices through open engagement with evidence (Mulnix, 2012). Given the array of information available and the need to investigate and note the voracity of differing sources; organisational ability based on sound background knowledge is a vital aspect of CT, according to Willingham (2008). This requires interpretation to help filter and categorise information as well as analytical skills to understand relationships between differing concepts and data. Indeed, Mulnix (2012) argues that inferencing ability is the underpinning skill of CT upon which all other related skills are dependent.

While ascertaining a truly objective standpoint may be untenable given these issues, this does not mean we should not stop striving to achieve as close to this goal as possible. Just because every source has some form of bias, this does mean that all sources are therefore equally valid. So, although in a democracy people's right to voice an opinion within the boundaries of the law should be respected, it does not therefore follow that we should have equal respect for all views and certainly not regard all views as being equally truthful or credible. Furthermore, objective understanding of an event is not necessarily somewhere in the middle of two contrasting viewpoints (Facione, 2015). Thus, the use of emotive anecdotes, however eloquently articulated, do not constitute reliable evidence, nor substantiate grandiose claims. Where demonstrable facts have been ignored, misinterpreted or selectively highlighted, or anecdotes used in place of substantive evidence, this shows that the source lacks credibility. In the case of an authoritative source, such an approach used would additionally suggest a lack of personal integrity. Opinions emanating from such work, as with all sources, should therefore be dispassionately challenged through use of robust and credible evidence (Hoffman, 2016). Therefore, when forming an opinion, what you should be seeking is articulation of the weight of robustly evidenced credible research.

Quantity by no means equals quality and with the internet, whatever information we are seeking, an overwhelming amount of data is available within seconds, generating too many sources to individually investigate. Digital literacy is therefore vital when performing internet searches; the first few sources may be present due to financial incentives being paid to the search engine provider rather than the voracity of their information. Similarly, other sources heading the queue may be present on the grounds of their popularity rather than the quality of the resource. Popularity is no guarantee of accuracy; Moon (2008) highlights Janis' concept of 'groupthink', where social compliance negates individuals' ability to think independently or question the underlying assumptions of the group:

> The more amiability and spirit de corps among the members of a policy-making in-group, the greater is the danger that independent critical thinking will be replaced by groupthink which is likely to lead to irrational and dehumanising actions directed against out-groups.
>
> (Janis, 1982, p 13, in Moon, 2008, p 9)

Similarly, within online media, 'echo chambers', or 'bubble worlds', where groups of likeminded individuals repeat and develop similar viewpoints, reinforce prejudices as they do not access robust evidence that may contradict their ever deeper engrained worldview (Peters, 2017). Additionally, glossy reports, often from commercial organisations or politically motivated think-tanks, may be easy to read, offering logical sounding solutions, but these are rarely peer-reviewed, meaning that evidence could be withheld, misused or misinterpreted to support the organisation's underlying agenda (Hoffman,

2016). Although peer-reviewed academic journal articles should reflect a higher academic standard if from a reputable journal, scepticism should be retained. If a view is based on experience, the long-term reflections of a recognised authority within a field of knowledge may have credibility. However, Hoffman (2016) warns that when academics speak beyond their field of knowledge within their professional capacity (rather than expressing a democratic right of voicing personal opinions) they damage their overall credibility. Furthermore, bias in scope of research, implementation and analysis, 'cherry picking' of selective data to support an argument as well as under or misrepresentation of conflicting evidence are all possible misuses of research (see Chapter 9). Even if you have obtained robust evidence about an issue, consider whether any elements of data are missing that will inform you of additional study needs. Additionally, research findings only ever represent the author's interpretation at the time of publication; subsequent academic study may substantiate, develop or challenge findings. Finally, for all sources, Moon (2008) highlights the need to identify explicit or implicit intentions of authors as well as consider how their context may have influenced approaches, scope and findings.

Forming and using judgements

People perceive truths in the face of contrary evidence due to personal circumstances, prejudices, motivations and beliefs; attempting to acknowledge how this influences your understanding is an important aspect of CT as it helps you understand the limitations of your judgement (Piro and Anderson, 2015). Piro and Anderson (2015) therefore note that collaborative approaches may help to question and challenge personal assumptions, though there remains the danger of 'groupthink' if using close colleagues.

Hoffman (2016) warns against critical investigations as an intellectual pursuit, arguing that a crucial role of an academic is to engage in public discourse to publicise findings to help create evidence-based change as an antidote to ill-informed opinion:

> *Academic and scientific communities have been ineffective or disengaged in explaining the state and gravity of scientific findings… For the benefit of society's ability to make wise decisions and for the benefit of the academy's ability to remain relevant, the academic community needs to accept its role in public engagement.*

(Hoffman, 2016, p 4)

However, Hoffman (2016) warns that presentation opens the critical thinker to criticisms of methods and findings. Where supported by relevant evidence, criticisms should not be viewed as failure but an opportunity to change judgement on the grounds of new evidence. This is not always easy; where hard work, personal values and professional reputation are at stake, admitting mistakes or omissions is difficult. However, to use evidence sparingly solely for the purpose of supporting your viewpoint or dismissing the claims of others is tantamount to dishonesty, regardless of how eloquently the argument is presented. It is therefore important not to overstate claims; ensure findings are well-supported by evidence and the investigation's limitations are clear. Admitting that findings are inconclusive or unsupportive of an issue are valid; evidence showing the necessity for further research or ceasing ineffective practice should be considered equally important to conclusions that advocate new approaches. Ultimately, Moon (2008) concludes that CT must provide evidence to inform ensuing action. Hoffman concurs, arguing that such evidence should actively inform open public debate:

> *The engaged scholar must recognize the extent to which discourse is inherently a dialogue rather than a monologue, a conversation requiring mutual respect and appreciation for the expertise of all sides. In order to succeed, academics need to accept that they do not have a monopoly on knowledge and expertise, and that engagement is a two-way learning process. This is a model of engagement based on service that entails reaching out to the community and making the effort to discover what issues matter to them, what they need to know or what help they need so that we can collectively address these issues.*
>
> (Hoffman, 2016, p 10)

Activity

Look at an education policy, such as the current focus on increasing academically selective schooling, *Schools that Work for Everyone* (DfE, 2016).

o   Who supports the idea? Who opposes? Who takes a more nuanced or even neutral stance?

o   What are the key arguments for and against the proposal?

o   To what extent are views based on anecdote or evidence? How robust is the evidence presented?

o   Considering the above, where do you consider the weight of robust, authoritative evidence lies?

o   If you are reading this after implementation, evaluate the extent to which proponents' or opponents' viewpoints at the time have been subsequently supported by evidence.

CRITICAL THINKING AND PROFESSIONAL PRACTICE

Critical thinking and teacher standards

Writing for the Welsh Assembly, educationalist Donaldson (2014) highlights links between CT and the ability to adapt to rapidly changing employer needs in a globalised economy. Former Conservative education secretary Baker (2016) concurs, listing it as a key curriculum aim for learners' employability. Piro and Anderson (2015) argue that CT should therefore be a central value of teacher education, citing progressive educationalist John Dewey's view that teachers should facilitate the development of socially responsible democratic citizens. With education being a devolved power of the elected assemblies within the UK, each nation has its own education professional standards. These give differing considerations of the role of CT, implying differing perceptions of the educator's role. For Scotland and Northern Ireland, critical questioning and challenging of government policy is central to the teacher's role in their mandatory standards:

> *Professionalism also implies the need to ask critical questions of educational policies and practices and to examine our attitudes and beliefs.*
>
> (GTCS, 2012 p 5)

> *the reflective and activist practitioner who, individually and collectively, will reflect on the nature and purposes of education, and will seek to act as both a shaper of policy and a well-informed critic of proposals and reforms.*
>
> (GTCNI, 2011, p 9)

Scotland and Northern Ireland see CT as central to personal and professional development by challenging assumptions and established practices, forming constructive criticality with colleagues and being able to, *critically evaluate a range of appropriate educational and research literature* (CTCS, 2012, p 18). The expectation here, linking education to informed citizenship and democracy, is that teachers should contribute to policy formation rather than blindly accept it. In contrast, the English and Welsh teacher standards, formulated by their respective governments, emphasise the importance of teachers understanding rather than challenging policy:

> *Teachers must have an understanding of, and always act within, the statutory frameworks which set out their professional duties and responsibilities.*
>
> (DfE, 2014, p 1)

> *Understand the national education policy context in Wales and the Welsh Government's national priorities for education including Cwricwlwm Cymreig to inform and shape their practice.*
>
> (Welsh Government, 2011, p 3)

The Welsh standards do not specifically mention CT, although personal reflection to improve practice is repeatedly advocated (Welsh Government, 2011). However, following general acceptance of the *Successful Futures* report on Welsh Education (Donaldson, 2014), the strong emphasis on the need for teachers to embed critical thinking throughout the curriculum may impact on subsequent iterations of these standards. Conversely, the only mention of CT in the English Teachers' Standards refers to being self-critical; instead the focus is on the importance of subject knowledge and regulatory compliance (DfE, 2014, p 1). However, the non-statutory English FE standards, from the Education and Training Foundation, emphasise the importance of CT for challenging viewpoints, although not going as far as challenging policy:

> *Teachers and trainers are **reflective** and **enquiring** practitioners who think **critically** about their own educational assumptions, values and practice in the context of a changing contemporary and educational world. They draw on relevant research as part of **evidence-based practice**.*
>
> (ETF, 2014, p 1, emphasis in original)

Teaching critical thinking

Mulnix (2012) argues that CT can be explicitly taught, emphasising the need for students to be made aware of its importance as it encourages rationality over prejudice. She concludes that as well as instruction on CT theory, teachers need to repeatedly model it in practice and show exemplars of strong and weak inferential reasoning. Specifically, Mulnix (2012) advocates mapping arguments to help develop inferential skills and evidential relationships as well as self and peer-assessment of work. The Welsh *Successful Futures* plan for improvement emphasises the importance of embedding critical thinking, as well as other high-level skills such as creativity and problem-solving, arguing that this is found in high performing education systems:

> *The demand for young people with improved levels of literacy, numeracy and wider skills, including critical thinking, creativity and problem solving, has fuelled an international trend towards curricula that give greater emphasis to the development of skills, alongside, or embedded in, a traditional subject or 'area of learning' approach.*
>
> (Donaldson, 2014, p 7)

However, English school standards minister Nick Gibb rejects the conclusions of the Organisation for Economic Co-operation and Development (OECD) on what works in education, instead personally interpreting their data as supporting knowledge-based curricula (Gibb, 2017). He therefore justifies the English adherence to a knowledge focus, based on the research and philosophy of E D Hirsch and cognitive scientists such as Willingham (2008). They emphasize the importance of learning key facts as an essential precursor to developing higher order skills; only with this overarching focus will learners be able to understand any concept sufficiently to develop criticality. Willingham therefore argues that CT can only be domain-specific rather than a generic transferable skill:

> *You can teach students maxims about how they ought to think, but without background knowledge and practice, they probably will not be able to implement the advice they memorize. Just as it makes no sense to try to teach factual content without giving students opportunities to practice using it, it also makes no sense to try to teach critical thinking devoid of factual content.*
>
> (Willingham, 2008, p 10)

Willingham's (2008) support for knowledge-focused learning is inspiring English education policy, being one of the few academic citations in the 2016 White Paper *Educational Excellence Everywhere*:

> *This cognitive science formed the background to the new, more ambitious national curriculum published in 2013. It sets out a core body of knowledge in a format designed to maximise pupil understanding and minimise confusion.*
>
> (DfE, 2016, p 89)

However, Mulnix (2012) warns against taking a subject-specific focus, as it implies that CT approaches are also domain-specific rather than having universal principles, thereby limiting inter-disciplinary inferences which could provide broader, and potentially more enlightening, connections. Hoffman (2016) concurs, arguing that overspecialisation in research can lead to a loss of relevance and failure to effectively contribute to public discourse. Finally, Mulnix (2012) reminds the critical thinker that taking a consistent approach to CT also means being continually informed and developed by ongoing CT teaching research to inform our practice.

LIMITATIONS OF CRITICAL THINKING

Mulnix (2012) rejects a tendency among academics to regard CT having primacy within a hierarchy of thinking skills, arguing that other forms of high-level thinking such as problem-solving, creative thinking and decision-making may be more suitable in differing situations. Higgins (2014) concurs, emphasising the importance of creative/imaginative thinking where innovation or conceptual exploration is required. In this context, CT could be a disadvantage, with a rational viewpoint hindering potentially groundbreaking insight, innovation or entrepreneurialism (Moore, 2013). Moon (2008) also emphasises the necessity of being able to draw upon experience to act quickly, such as when engaged in teaching and then engaging more in-depth reflective and CT skills after the event to help plan future improvement. Finally, Mulnix (2012) warns against equating CT with moral virtue, claiming that where guidance advocates that CT should be committed to a sense of justice or social cause, it ceases to be an intellectual virtue:

> *Two critical thinkers can come to hold contrary beliefs despite each applying the skills associated with CT well and honestly... It is a theory about how to think, not about how to live.*

(Mulnix, 2012, pp 466–7)

SUMMARY OF KEY POINTS

o   Presenting your work articulately and transparently is important for your findings to be considered and taken seriously as an academic.

o   Eloquence should not be mistaken for integrity; retain a sceptical and questioning approach for all sources.

o   Evidence-based findings are often complex, nuanced and are therefore less attractive-sounding than simple sloganeering or solutions. CT therefore requires resilience and persistence.

o   CT requires reflexivity, acknowledging that no one, including ourselves, is without limitations, areas of ignorance and preconceptions; becoming a critical thinker is therefore a lifelong journey of personal development.

Check your understanding

1   What are the benefits of critical thinking?

2   What are the limitations?

3   Why is critical thinking important for your personal, academic and professional practice?

4   Identify where CT is required in your course objectives, content and assessments.

5   How is CT defined by your course/institution?

6   Compare this definition with viewpoints covered in this chapter.

 TAKING IT FURTHER

Cottrell, S (2011) *Critical Thinking Skills: Developing Effective Analysis and Argument.* London: Palgrave. Practical guidance to help you develop your critical thinking ability.

Staffordshire University (2017) *Critical Thinking.* [Online]. Retrieved from: http://libguides.staffs.ac.uk/critical_thinking (accessed 23 April 2017). A basic introduction to critical thinking for HE study.

REFERENCES

Baker, K (2016) *14–19 Education: A New Baccalaureate.* London: The Edge Foundation. [Online]. Retrieved from: www.edge.co.uk/research/research-reports/14-19-education-a-new-baccalaureate (accessed 23 April 2017).

DfE (2014) *Teachers' Standards.* [Online]. Retrieved from: www.gov.uk/government/publications/teachers-standards (accessed 23 April 2017).

DfE (2016). *Educational Excellence Everywhere.* London: HMSO.

Donaldson, G (2014) *Successful Futures: Independent Review of Curriculum and Assessment Arrangements in Wales.* [Online]. Available from: http://gov.wales/topics/educationandskills/schoolshome/curriculum-for-wales-curriculum-for-life/why-we-are-changing/successful-futures/?lang=en (accessed 23 April 2017).

Elder, L and Paul, R (2010) *The Thinker's Guide to Analytic Thinking,* 2nd edition. Tomales, California: Foundation for Critical Thinking.

ETF (2014) *Professional Standards for Teachers and Trainers: England*. [Online]. Retrieved from: www.et-foundation.co.uk/supporting/support-practitioners/professional-standards (accessed 23 April 2017).

Facione, P (2015) *Critical Thinking: What It Is and Why It Counts*. Henmosa Beach, California: California Academic Press. [Online]. Retrieved from: www.insightassessment.com/About-Us/Measured-Reasons/pdf-file/Critical-Thinking-What-It-Is-and-Why-It-Counts-PDF (accessed 23 April 2017).

GCTNI (2011) *Teaching: The Reflective Profession. Professional Competencies*, 3rd edition. [Online]. Retrieved from: www.gtcni.org.uk/index.cfm/area/information/page/profstandard (accessed 23 April 2017).

Gibb, N (2017) *The Evidence in Favour of Teacher-Led Instruction*. [Online]. Retrieved from: www.gov.uk/government/speeches/nick-gibb-the-evidence-in-favour-of-teacher-led-instruction (accessed 23 April 2017).

GTCS (2012) *The Standards for Registration: Mandatory Requirements for Registration with the General Teaching Council for Scotland*. [Online]. Retrieved from: www.gtcs.org.uk/professional-standards/professional-standards.aspx (accessed 23 April 2017).

Higgins, S (2014) Critical Thinking for 21st Century Education: A Cyber-Tooth Curriculum? Durham: *UNESCO IBE*.

Hoffman, A (2016) Reflections: Academia's Emerging Crisis of Relevance and the Consequent Role of the Engaged Scholar. *Journal of Change Management*, 16(2): 1–20.

Moon, J (2008) *Critical Thinking: An Exploration of Theory and Practice*. Oxon: Routledge.

Moore, T (2013) Critical Thinking: Seven Definitions of a Concept. *Studies in Higher Education*, 38(4): 506–22.

Mulnix, J (2012) Thinking Critically about Critical Thinking. *Educational Philosophy and Theory*, 44(5): 464–79.

Peters, M (2017) Education in a Post-Truth World. *Educational Philosophy and Theory*, 49(1): 1–4.

Piro, J and Anderson, G (2015) Discussions in a Socrates Café: Implications for Critical Thinking in Teacher Education. *Action in Teacher Education*, 37(3): 265–83.

QAA (2015) *Subject Benchmark Statement: Education Studies*. [Online]. Retrieved from: www.qaa.ac.uk/publications/information-and-guidance/publication?PubID=2916#.WKljkPnyjic (accessed 23 April 2017).

Sky News (2016) *EU: In or Out?* [Online]. Retrieved from: www.youtube.com/watch?v=t8D8AoC-5i8 (accessed 23 April 2017).

Vaughn, L (2015) *The Power of Critical Thinking: Effective Reasoning about Ordinary and Extraordinary Claims*, 5th edition. Oxford: Oxford University Press.

Welsh Government (2011) *Revised Professional Standards for Education Practitioners in Wales*. [Online]. Retrieved from: http://learning.gov.wales/resources/collections/professional-standards?lang=en (accessed 23 April 2017).

Willingham, D (2008) Critical Thinking: Why is it So Hard to Teach? *Arts Education Policy Review*, 109(4): 8–19.

The historical context of English education (1988–the present)

Types of schools

Education Act (1996)

Strategies for raising social mobility: Pupil Premium

Compulsory and post-compulsory education

An overview of key education policies

Changes to initial teacher education

Evaluating social mobility strategies

Competition and change to initial teacher education

Education Reform Act (1988)

The historical context of English education

Quality assurance inspectorates

The national curriculum and standardisation of practices

Who controls education?

Key educational policy drivers

Apprenticeships, Skills, Children and Learning Act (2009)

Education and Skills Act (2008)

INTRODUCTION

This chapter's focus is on outlining a historical account of reforms from the 1988 Education Reform Act. Your views about your school days and the type of education you received will be influenced by your age and the type of school and/or college you attended, and your views might be significantly different to those of your peers, family or friends. This is because policy plays a significant part in shaping the way educational institutions deliver programmes of learning as well as how they manage learners' well-being.

SUBJECT EXPERTISE LINKS

This chapter helps you work towards the following QAA (2015) *Subject Benchmark Statement: Education Studies* standards.

Knowledge and understanding

o   The underlying values, theories and concepts relevant to education.

o   The societal and organisational structures and purposes of educational systems, and the possible implications for learners and the learning process.

Application

o   Analyse educational concepts, theories and issues of policy in a systematic way.

o   Use of a range of evidence to formulate appropriate and justified ways forward and potential changes in practice.

Reflection

o   The ability to reflect on their own and others' value systems.

OBJECTIVES

This chapter develops your understanding of:

o   key education policies and their impact on teachers, learners and learning for schools and further education;

o   who controls education;

o   key education policy drivers;

o   deregulation and competition in education;

o   the national curriculum and standardisation of practices;

o   social mobility strategies.

AN OVERVIEW OF KEY EDUCATION POLICIES

Drivers for education reform usually occur for one or more of the following reasons:

○   a sense that 'something must be done';

○   ideology – the values and beliefs of policy makers;

○   international exemplars;

○   cost;

○   electoral popularity;

○   pressure groups;

○   personal experience;

○   research evidence.

(Perry et al., 2010, p 3)

However, whatever the reason for wanting reform, all requests for legislative change have to go through a systematic process; usually following the example given in Table 2.1.

Table 2.1 Legislative process

Term	Meaning
Green Paper	A consultation paper that usually precedes a White Paper.
White Paper	A paper that is presented by the government department to which it relates, i.e., the Department for Education. It provides information or proposals on an issue. It feeds into a Bill.
Bill	A Bill is a draft of an intended law.
Act of Parliament	Acts provide a new or amended law.

Some policies and laws implemented by the government will apply to all of the UK whereas other policies will apply to either Scotland, England, Wales, Northern Ireland or a combination of two or more of these. For example, each country in the UK has their own policy relating to the age at which children are required to receive and to remain in compulsory education.

Compulsory and post-compulsory education

Compulsory education is generally provided in a school setting whereas post-compulsory education is usually provided in a further education college, university or training organisations. (Post-compulsory education is discussed in more detail in Chapter 7.)

Types of schools

Most children in the UK attend school to receive a formal education. Most attend one or more of the schools listed below (Chapter 6 provides more information about types of schools):

○   Primary and secondary state schools. These offer free education to all children. They follow the national curriculum.

○   Grammar schools. These are run by the council, a foundation body or a trust. Children are selected to attend these schools based on their academic ability and there is often an examination to get in. They follow the national curriculum.

○   Faith schools. These are run by a governing body. They follow the national curriculum but, within certain parameters, have a choice about what they teach in religious studies. They often have different entry criteria to state schools.

○   Independent/private schools. These schools charge tuition fees. They don't have to follow the national curriculum.

○   Special schools. These schools provide education for children with specific educational need/s (SEN).

○   Academies. These are run by a governing body or multi-academy trusts (MATs). Within certain parameters they can design their own curriculum.

Since the Academies Act was introduced in 2010 there has been a steady growth in the number of schools changing to academy status.

Changes to the structure of schools and the introduction of academies

City Academies were established, at a time of a Labour government, through the Learning and Skills Act in 2000. Following on from the introduction of these, the Education Act, 2002 rebadged them to become Sponsored Academies with the purpose of replacing *under-performing schools with the aim of improving educational standards and raising the aspirations of, and career prospects for, pupils from all backgrounds including the most disadvantaged* (Politics UK, 2017, p 3).

Eight years later the then Coalition government introduced the Academies Act (2010) and opportunities for *successful schools to convert to academies in order to benefit from the increased autonomy academy status brings* (Politics UK, 2017, p 4).

Academies are state-funded but independent schools overseen by not-for-profit businesses, known as academy trusts. Academies have to abide by the same rules as state schools with regards to admissions, inclusivity and equality. However, they have more autonomy in their design of a curriculum providing this includes English, mathematics, science and religious education and they need to comply with national standards regarding testing pupils' achievements (Kauko and Salokangas, 2015).

In 2016, a White Paper, (commissioned by Nicky Morgan, education secretary), *Educational Excellence Everywhere*, recommended that all schools should become academies by 2020. The paper also recommended that by 2022, local authorities should cease to maintain schools and that the majority of schools will be managed by multi-academy trusts (MATs); the rationale for this being to maximise funding efficiencies through shared resources and to also support the development through CPD of the quality of teaching and learning (DfE, 2016).

However, following controversy about this policy, Nicky Morgan reviewed it and announced that schools could continue to have a choice whether to become an academy or not. Furthermore, for all their increasing popularity, academies are not always successful. Statistically they are achieving at a lower level than local authority maintained schools (Stewart, 2013) and there has been no significant change in the position of UK schools in the Programme for International Student Assessment (PISA) rankings (for more information about this see Chapter 8).

Furthermore, policy can often be usurped by unexpected changes; not least, a new prime minister and a new education secretary in 2016 swiftly followed by the March budget and the triggering of Brexit in 2017; all of which could influence a change in the future of academies and how education is managed.

Activity

Source some recent articles about academies and consider how recent changes to the UK's political landscape are shaping the future of academies.

Education Act (1996)

Before 1988 (the focus of this chapter) there were several pivotal Acts of Parliament passed; all instrumental in the raising of the school leaving age (ROSLA). You may find it useful to do some background reading about some of these Acts, for example:

○   1870 Elementary Education Act;

○   1918 Fisher Education Act;

○   1944 Butler Education Act.

Currently, the school leaving age for children in the UK is 16 (although the participation in education age is 18). There is some variation in Scotland, England, Wales and Northern Ireland regarding at which point during a child's 16th birthday they can leave school.

Activity

Which Acts in England, Wales, Scotland and Northern Ireland have influenced the raising of the school leaving age since 1988?

Education Reform Act (1988)

The Education Reform Act was instrumental in changing the landscape of education in several ways. One significant way was by the introduction of the national curriculum.

Activity

What were some other key features of the Education Reform (1988) Act?

THE NATIONAL CURRICULUM AND STANDARDISATION OF PRACTICES

Following much debate at ministerial level, the Education Reform Act (1988) established a national curriculum, which set out what should be taught and assessed in schools so that all children of school age received the same standard of education. Most state schools in England and Wales are required to comply with the requirements of this curriculum. Similarly, Scotland have a Curriculum for Excellence programme and Northern Ireland have a Common Curriculum. Other types of schools (for example, academies and private schools) design and deliver their own curricula.

The aim of the national curriculum was, and is, to:

o   promote the spiritual, moral, cultural, mental and physical development of pupils, and to prepare pupils for the opportunities, responsibilities and experiences of adult life.

o   be structured around Key Stages and be subject-based.

o   provide a syllabus for each subject at each Key Stage which would also include a scale of attainment targets to guide teacher assessment.

(DCSF, 2009)

Following several reviews of the national curriculum changes have been made, for example:

1993   Following complaints by teachers a revised national curriculum was rolled out in 1995.

1996   Support projects were introduced in order to improve the teaching of literacy and numeracy in primary schools.

1997   The support projects were modified and became known as the National Literacy and Numeracy Strategies. These National Literacy and Numeracy Strategies were rolled out to secondary schools.

2009   Unpopular standard attainment tests (SATs) for 14 year olds are scrapped, along with the science exam for 11 year olds.

(Collins, 2011)

In October 2013, and again in 2014, the Department for Education (DfE) published further changes to the national curriculum; these were:

o   Changes to English and mathematics curricula for pupils in Years 2, 6 and 10 from September 2015, and for pupils in Year 11 from September 2016.

○ Changes to the science curriculum will come into force for Year 10 pupils in September 2016, and Year 11 pupils in September 2017.

(DfE, 2017)

Following recommendations made in the Donaldson report in 2015 to review the assessment and curriculum, Wales is rolling out a new curriculum for delivery in 2018.

Activity

Locate the curriculum for Scotland, England, Wales and Northern Ireland and discuss the similarities and variations between them. Why are these variations necessary?

Education and Skills Act (2008)

The Education and Skills Act (2008) introduced a new *participation age* – this is different from the school leaving age, which remains at 16. Through this Act, the age that children in England are required to *participate* in some form of formal education or training has increased. This increase was staggered and between 2013 and 2015 children needed to be in some form of training or education until they turned 17; after 2015 this age was raised to 18. (gov.co.uk, 2017)

The incremental increases to the raising of the school leaving age and the raising of the participation age have not been without criticism. According to Politics UK there exists some:

> scepticism that the school leaving age is increased at times when the government wishes to reduce the number of young people seeking employment, and thereby increasing the unemployment statistics.

(Politics UK, 2017, p 1)

Children can continue to participate either part- or full-time in their formal education by, for example, attending a sixth form college, a further education college or a private training organisation. They can also belong to an apprenticeship scheme and develop subject-specific skills and knowledge through on-the-job training. Apprenticeship schemes have, in some format, always existed but in 2009 a new Act outlined proposals for a new apprenticeship scheme.

Apprenticeships, Skills, Children and Learning Act (2009)

The Apprenticeships, Skills, Children and Learning Act (2009) outlined the provision and necessary legislative requirements for training young people aged 16 to 18 as well as some people up to the age of 25 (for example, young offenders serving time in a prison and for some learners with special educational needs). This Act places funding for education and training for these young people with local authorities rather than the Learning and Skills Council (LSC).

However, by 2012, and with a change in government from Labour to a Coalition (Conservative and Liberal Democrat), a review of apprenticeships was undertaken. This review recommended:

o   effective and trusted qualifications;

o   accomplishments must be robustly tested and validated;

o   maths and English to be taught in a real world context.

(Richard, 2012, pp 6–9)

More changes with regards to apprenticeships are imminent. Specifically, during 2017 some employers will contribute to an apprenticeship levy.

Activity

Find two newspaper articles that present differing views on the current proposals for an apprenticeship levy.

KEY EDUCATIONAL POLICY DRIVERS

Since 1988 some of the key policies that have influenced change within education are outlined in Table 2.2.

Table 2.2 Key education policies

Date	Title	Comments
1988	Education Reform Act	This Act brought about significant reforms including the implementation of a national curriculum for primary and secondary state schools in England, Wales and Northern Ireland.
1994	Teacher Training Agency established	This Agency was tasked with providing advice about teaching and also to provide funding for training for teachers in order to raise teaching standards.
1996	Education Act	This Act changed the raising of the school leaving age for all young people to the last Friday in June during the year in which they were 16.
1997	Qualifications and Curriculum Authority	Qualifications and Curriculum Authority replaces School Curriculum and Assessment Authority and the National Council for Vocational Qualifications.
1998	General Teaching Council established	This Council was established to improve the standards of teaching in schools. It was dissolved in 2012.
2000	Learning and Skills Act	This Act established City Academies.
2002	Education Act	City Academies became academies.
2006	Leitch Report Prosperity for all in the global economy – world-class skills.	The review set out strategies for the UK to become a world leader on skills by 2020.

Date	Title	Comments
2008	DfES, Raising Expectations: Enabling the system to deliver	This White Paper introduced recommendations for the raising of the participation age; first to 17 and then to 18.
2008	The Education and Skills Act	This Act followed on from the Raising Expectations paper. It stipulated the requirements of a new participation age.
2009	Apprenticeships, Skills, Children and Learning Act 2009	This Act outlined the provision and necessary legislative requirements for training young people aged 16 to 18 and some young people up to the age of 25.
2010	The Importance of Teaching	This White Paper made recommendations for improving the quality of teaching and learning.
2010	Academies Act	This Act, by introducing a different type of school, brought about change to the educational offering for young people in the UK.
2010	Training our next generation of outstanding teachers	This initial teacher education strategy recommended that more training should take place in schools and that graduates should be of the highest quality.
2011	Education Act	This Act changed current areas of educational policy, including the school staff ability to discipline learners, qualifications regulations, the provision of post-16 education, including vocational apprenticeships, student finance for higher education.
2011	Education Strategy 2020	This strategy focused on the quality of teacher training and its ability to equip learners with the skills necessary to work and to compete in a global economy.
2011	The Wolf Report	This report recommended changes to vocational education.
2012	Richard Review of Apprenticeships	This review looked at the current models of apprenticeships and how they should be developed in the future and in line with a changing economy.
2015	Government policy: Teaching and school leadership	This policy made recommendations for improving the quality of teaching and learning.
2016	Educational Excellence Everywhere	This White Paper presented recommendations for reforms in schools.

Activity

Which, if any, of the policies in Table 2.2 have had a direct impact on the education provision delivered at your organisation and/or in your own practice? For what reasons?

WHO CONTROLS EDUCATION?

The UK government controls education. However, parliamentary divisions in Scotland, England, Wales and Northern Ireland provide some variations to this control, particularly with regards to quality assurance inspectorates and other professional bodies.

Activity

What decisions might the government make with regards to compulsory education? What might influence these decisions?

Quality assurance inspectorates

Although, there are different quality assurance bodies for Scotland, England, Wales and Northern Ireland, all of them have a similar remit – to inspect and to quality assure providers of formal education. Inspectors visit schools, colleges and other education institutions and using criteria provided within their inspection framework inspect the quality of teaching and learning, leadership and management and, based on their findings, provide a judgement and make recommendations for improvement.

Ofsted (England)

Prior to 1992 schools were inspected by Her Majesty's Inspectorate (HMI). Following the 1992 Education (Schools) Act, the Office for Standards in Education (Ofsted) became responsible for inspecting schools in England, which in 2007 was broadened to include the work by children's services relating to social care and Her Majesty's Court Services (HMCS). In order to reflect this addition, Ofsted's name was changed to the Office for Standards in Education, Children's Services and Skills. With its power to close down ineffective schools, Ofsted has often been criticised and Whitty notes that it is *doubtful if a more ambitious programme of school-by-school evaluation and review has ever been mounted anywhere in the world* (Whitty, 2008, p 170). (You will find more information about Ofsted in Chapter 6.)

Her Majesty's Inspectorate of Education (Scotland)

Until 2011, the Scottish education provision was inspected by Her Majesty's Inspectorate of Education (HMIe). In 2011, following a merger with Learning and Teaching, Scotland, the inspectorate became known as Education Scotland.

Estyn (Wales)

Estyn (meaning *reach out*) is led by Her Majesty's Chief Inspector of Education and Training in Wales and is the body responsible for inspecting education provision in Wales.

The Education and Training Inspectorate (Northern Ireland)

The Northern Ireland education system is inspected by the Education and Training Inspectorate (ETI). The ETI provide independent inspection services and policy advice for the Department of Education.

Activity

Look at the last two inspection reports completed for the educational institution where you work or are studying. Alternatively look at an inspection report for a school or college within the area you live.

○   What are three key findings in these reports?

○   What might be some reasons for similarities or differences within these reports?

As well as inspectorate bodies (Ofsted, HMIe, Estyn, ETI), there are other regulatory and professional bodies that have significant influence and control with regards to the way in which schools, colleges and other education providers function. For example, the Department for Education is responsible for children's services and education, including higher and further education policy, apprenticeships and wider skills in England.

Activity

○   Do you belong to a professional body?

○   If so, what is its remit?

Some professional bodies have more longevity than others. The General Teaching Council for Scotland (GTCS) and the General Teaching Council for Northern Ireland (GTCNI) still exist, but the General Teaching Council for England (GTCE) was dissolved in 2012 when the Teaching Agency (an executive agency of the Department for Education) took over some of the roles of the GTCE. In 2013, the Teaching Agency became the National College for Teaching and Leadership.

COMPETITION AND CHANGE TO INITIAL TEACHER EDUCATION

As the Red Queen told Alice, *it takes all the running you can do, to keep in the same place* (Lewis Carroll, *Through the Looking-Glass*, 1871). While some may argue that the flotilla of policies surrounding education is too much, too quick (Norris and Adam, 2017), the emergence of them has gathered increasingly more momentum over the past few decades due to fast-changing political, social, technological and global environments.

Standing still is not an option and running to keep pace with regional, national and global competitors is a constant consideration for heads of schools, senior management and politicians charged with overseeing education and initiating appropriate policy. Arguably – and the constant flurry of educational policies support this argument – running faster (or more efficiently) is crucial to the UK's drive to maintain and grow its position in global market and education league tables such as those presented in the PISA rankings. However, so far, regardless of the significant financial contributions provided by the government to implement new initiatives to improve the quality of teaching (Institute for Fiscal Studies, 2015) there has been little improvement over in the UK's PISA (2015) rankings (Kuczera et al., 2016). (You will find further information about PISA rankings and education within a global perspective in Chapter 8.)

Changes to initial teacher education

Compared to its post-compulsory counterparts (see Chapter 7), how and who delivers teacher education within the schools sector has remained relatively stable. Traditionally delivered within a university academic setting, new models of delivery have emerged during the past decade – for example, Schools Direct and Graduate Teaching programmes – and according to recommendations made in a White Paper (DfE, 2016) the emphasis on school-based, on-the-job training is likely to increase. This White Paper also promotes a longer period of teacher training accreditation; a notion later supported by the education secretary Justine Greening, who has suggested the *introduction of a newly strengthened QTS from September 2019* (Greening, 2017). However, this proposed vocational model, with as little as 30 days scheduled into its curriculum for academic study at a university, runs contrary to many teacher training models in some European countries; some of which have four or five years of academic study, with a pedagogical dimension included but for relatively brief periods (Brown, 2016, p 2).

EVALUATING SOCIAL MOBILITY STRATEGIES

An approach used in England, and similarly replicated as appropriate in Scotland, Wales and Northern Ireland, to measure social mobility through education is by:

1. *Performance of disadvantaged pupils in early years test*

2. *Performance of disadvantaged pupils in Key Stage 2 tests*

3. *Performance of disadvantaged pupils at GCSE*

4. *Progress of non-privileged/disadvantaged pupils to universities*

5. *Progress of non-privileged graduates to professional occupations*

(Sutton Trust, 2015, p 1)

Tests might measure social mobility but they do not find solutions to raising pupils' social mobility. A report by Ofsted in 2013 found that in 1993 some young people felt disadvantaged within school and also when trying to gain employment due to their (low-status) geographical location and address. Twenty years later, the report notes that through some improvements in education there had been impact on disadvantaged youngsters; however, this was slow. As a way forward this report recommends;

○ *being tougher with schools; including re-inspection if they are seen as letting poorer pupils down;*

○ *fully implementing the Richard Review of apprenticeships.*

(Ofsted, 2013)

Activity

Give examples of some of the reasons for social mobility policies not having the impact intended.

Strategies for raising social mobility: Pupil Premium

With social mobility, equality and inclusivity in mind, one significant strategy introduced by Michael Gove, education secretary, in 2011 was additional funding through the provision of a Pupil Premium for pupils who need it the most.

However, Alexandra (2016) suggests that Pupil Premium widens rather than narrows the gap as:

> *teachers commonly refer to Pupil Premium pupils as though such a group can be defined meaningfully, when in fact it consists of no more than a highly diverse aggregation of individuals whose only common feature is that they have free school meals.*

(Alexandra, 2016, p 8)

Activity

Give examples of other strategies that the government, or a school that you know of, have implemented in order to raise the social mobility of pupils.

Education secretary Justin Greening remarked in a speech in January 2017 that *education has the power to transform lives and to improve social mobility.* However, where there is a *failure to set out and monitor long-term strategy and plans adequately* (Norris and Adams, 2017), how this is actually achieved is continually being debated.

Activity

○ What changes has the March 2017 budget had on education, in particular where you work and for you personally?

○ What impact might Brexit have on education, in particular where you work and for you personally?

SUMMARY OF KEY POINTS

Education needs to continually evolve to meet changing economic, social and technological needs. It is these needs that drive changes in policy.

o   Policy is instrumental to changes in who delivers formal education.

o   Policy is instrumental to changes in how formal education is delivered.

o   Policy is instrumental in shaping how teachers are trained to provide quality teaching and learning.

o   Policy is instrumental in shaping how funding is allocated to subjects, courses, infrastructure, human resources, technology and buildings.

Looking at the history of education, and understanding some of the reasons for the decisions made, helps policy-makers and stakeholders in education to shape the future of education. With Brexit on the horizon, doing this has, arguably, never been more important.

 Check your understanding

1   What age can a child leave school?

2   Who controls education?

3   What is social mobility?

4   Why is there so much political emphasis on raising the quality of teaching and learning?

 TAKING IT FURTHER

Butler Act (1944) *The Cabinet Papers 1915–1982*. [Online]. Retrieved from: www. nationalarchives.gov.uk/education/resources/attlees-britain/education-act-1944. Contains information about radical post-war changes to the UK's education system.

DfE (2015) *Academy and Free School Funding Agreement*. [Online]. Retrieved from: www.gov.uk/government/publications/academy-and-free-school-funding-agreements-single-academy-trust. Contains information about funding academies.

Department for Education (2016) Why do I need to attend school? [Online]. Retrieved from: www.education-ni.gov.uk/articles/why-do-i-need-attend-school#toc-0. Contains regulatory information and information about the purpose of schooling.

Gillard D. (n.d.) Education in England, the history of our schools. [Online] Retrieved from: www.educationengland.org.uk/documents/james (accessed 23 April 2017). Provides a brief history of education in England.

Office for Standards in Education, www.ofsted.gov.uk (accessed 23 April 2017). Ofsted contains contacts and inspection reports on many institutions, including schools and colleges. Provides information about education and skills in the UK.

The Apprenticeship, Skills, Children and Learning Act (2009) *Year 2015 to 16 – Detailed Guidance*. [Online]. Retrieved from: www.gov.uk/guidance/funding-initial-teacher-training-itt-academic-year-2015-to-16.

REFERENCES

Academies and Free Schools Fourth Report of Session 2014–15 (2015) [Online]. Retrieved from: www.publications.parliament.uk/pa/cm201415/cmselect/cmeduc/258/258.pdf (accessed 23 April 2017).

Adams, R, Weale, S, Bemgtsson, H and Carrell, S (6 December 2016) *UK Schools Fail to Climb International League Table*. [Online]. Retrieved from: www.theguardian.com/education/2016/dec/06/english-schools-core-subject-test-results-international-oecd-pisa (accessed 23 April 2017).

Alexandra, R (2016) *What Works and What Matters: Education in Spite of Policy*. [Online]. Retrieved from: www.robinalexander.org.uk/wp-content/uploads/2016/11/Alexander-CPRT-keynote-final1.pdf (accessed 23 April 2017).

Brown, T (2016) *The Beginnings of School-Led Teacher Training: New Challenges for University Teachers*. BERA Blog. [Online]. Retrieved from: www.bera.ac.uk/blog/the-beginnings-of-school-led-teacher-training-new-challenges-for-university-teacher-education (accessed 23 April 2017).

Chapman, C (2013) Academy Federations, Chains and Teaching Schools in England: Reflections on Leadership, Policy and Practice. *Journal of School Choice*, 7(3): 334–52.

Collins, N (2011) *How the National Curriculum Has Evolved*. [Online]. Retrieved from: www.telegraph.co.uk/education/educationnews/8270189/How-the-national-curriculum-has-evolved.html (accessed 23 April 2017).

DCSF (2008) *Raising Expectations, Expecting the System to Deliver*. [Online]. Retrieved from: www.gov.uk/government/uploads/system/uploads/attachment_data/file/238749/7348.pdf (accessed 23 April 2017).

DCSF (April 2009) *National Curriculum Fourth Report of Session 2008–2009, Vol 1*. Children Schools and Families Committee, House of Commons

DfE (2010a) *The Importance of Teaching: The Schools White Paper 2010*. London: HMSO.

DfE (2010b) *Training Our Next Generation of Outstanding Teachers*. London: HMSO.

DfE (2015) *2010 to 2015 Government Policy: Teaching and School Leadership*. [Online]. Retrieved from: www.gov.uk/government/publications/2010-to-2015-government-policy-teaching-and-school-leadership/2010-to-2015-government-policy-teaching-and-school-leadership (accessed 23 April 2017).

DfE (2016) *Educational Excellence Everywhere*. London: HMSO.

DfE (2017) *National Curriculum*. [Online]. Retrieved from: www.gov.uk (accessed 23 April 2017).

DfES (2008) *Raising Expectations: Enabling the System to Deliver*. [Online]. Retrieved from: www.education.gov.uk/consultations/downloadableDocs/Raising%20 Expectations%20pdf.pdf (accessed 23 April 2017).

Gov.co.uk (2017) *School Leaving Age*. [Online]. Retrieved from: www.gov.uk/know-when-you-can-leave-school (accessed 23 April 2017).

Greening, J (19 January 2017) *Education at the Core of Social Mobility*. [Online]. Retrieved from: www.gov.uk/government/speeches/justine-greening-education-at-the-core-of-social-mobility (accessed 23 April 2017).

Institute for Fiscal Studies (2015) *Education Spending*. [Online]. Retrieved from: www.ifs. org.uk/tools_and_resources/fiscal_facts/public_spending_survey/education (accessed 23 April 2017).

Kauko, J and Salokangas, M (2015) The Evaluation and Steering of English Academy Schools through Inspection and Examinations: National Visions and Local Practices. *British Educational Research Journal*, 41(6): 1108–24.

Kuczera, M, Field, S and Windisch, H (2016) *Building Skills for All: Survey of Adult Skills*. [Online]. Retrieved from: www.oecd.org/unitedkingdom/building-skills-for-all-review-of-england.pdf (accessed 23 April 2017).

Learning and Skills Act (2000) *Legislation Data*. [Online]. Retrieved from: www.legislation. gov.uk/ukpga/2000/21/contents (accessed 23 April 2017).

Norris, E and Adams, R (2017) *All Change: Why Britain is so Prone to Policy Reinvention, and What Can Be Done About It?* London: Institute for Government.

OECD (2017) *PISA 2015 Results*. [Online]. Retrieved from: www.oecd.org/pisa (accessed 23 April 2017).

Ofsted (2013) *Unseen Children: Access and Achievement 20 Years On: Evidence Report*. Manchester: Ofsted. [Online]. Retrieved from: www.gov.uk/government/uploads/system/uploads/attachment_data/file/379157/Unseen_20children_20-_20access_20and_20achievement_2020_20years_20on.pdf (accessed 23 April 2017).

Perry, A, Amadeo, C and Fletcher, M (2010) *Instinct or Reason: How Education Policy is Made and How We Might Make it Better*. Reading: CfBT Education Trust.

Politics UK (2017) *Education Leaving Age*. [Online]. Retrieved from: www.politics.co.uk/reference/education-leaving-age (accessed 23 April 2017).

QAA (2015) *Subject Benchmark Statement: Education Studies*. [Online]. Retrieved from: www.qaa.ac.uk/en/Publications/Documents/SBS-education-studies-15.pdf (accessed 23 April 2017).

Richard, D (2012) *Richard Review of Apprenticeships*. London: Department for Business Innovation and Skills. [Online]. Retrieved from: www.gov.uk/government/uploads/system/uploads/attachment_data/file/34708/richard-review-full.pdf (accessed 23 April 2017).

Stewart, H (2013) *Do Local Authorities Still Have a Role?* [Online]. Retrieved from: www.localschoolsnetwork.org.uk/2013/02/do-local-authorities-still-have-a-role (accessed 23 April 2017).

Sutton Trust (2015) *The Social Mobility Index*. [Online]. Retrieved from: www.suttontrust.com/researcharchive/mobility-map-background (accessed 23 April 2017).

Whitty, G (2008) Twenty Years of Progress? English Education Policy 1988 to the Present. *Educational Management Administration & Leadership*, 36(2): 165–84.

3 Current approaches to teaching, learning and assessment

INTRODUCTION

This chapter explores contemporary research and theories in relation to teaching, learning and assessment. It also critically examines the impact of underpinning ideology and government policy on these aspects, including the growing importance of maths, English/literacy and vocational skills within education

---

SUBJECT EXPERTISE LINKS

This chapter helps you work towards the following QAA (2015) *Subject Benchmark Statement: Education Studies* standards.

Knowledge and understanding

o   The complexity of the interaction between learning and local and global contexts, and the extent to which participants (including learners and teachers) can influence the learning process.

o   The underlying values, theories and concepts relevant to education.

Application

o   Analyse educational concepts, theories and issues of policy in a systematic way.

o   Accommodate new principles and understandings.

Reflection

o   The ability to use their knowledge and understanding critically to locate and justify a personal position in relation to the subject.

o   An understanding of the significance and limitations of theory and research.

OBJECTIVES

This chapter develops your understanding of current policy, ideology and theory in relation to:

o   effective teaching and learning;

o   lesson planning and preparation;

o   assessment;

o   mathematics, English/literacy and vocational skills within the curriculum.

EFFECTIVE TEACHING AND LEARNING

What is learning?

Learning is the core of education and the focus of all teaching professionals. At its simplest, learning can be viewed as an *'epistemic' or 'knowledge-building' activity* (Young, 2015, p 17). Illeris takes this further, commenting that *the concept of learning includes a very extensive and complicated set of processes* (2009, p 7). Whichever way learning is viewed, underlying theories are abundant, multifaceted and often interlinked. With theories ranging from those in relation to learning preferences, cognitive processing, variety, collaboration and engagement, the applications to professionals working in education can be many and varied.

UK government policy has in recent years moved strongly towards a knowledge-based curriculum, with the schools minister Nick Gibb recognising the influence of E Hirsch, a US academic who, he believes, provides *a compelling social justice case with which to argue for a knowledge-rich curriculum* (Gibb, 2015, p 14). Such focus on a knowledge-based curriculum was also advocated by former Secretary of State for Education, Michael Gove. However it has been heavily condemned by academics, culminating in a letter to the *Independent* in 2013 and making a number of criticisms of the content rich curriculum:

○ *This will put pressure on teachers to rely on rote learning without understanding*

○ *The new curriculum is extremely narrow*

○ *It demands too much too young*

(*Independent*, 2013)

However, learning can never be just about knowledge. Illeris suggests that learning can be considered in terms of *cognitive, social and emotional learning* (2003, p 399) and the notion of a social dimension is supported by Young who comments that *there is no learning (and no knowledge) that does not in some sense involve social relations* (2015, p 17).

---

1. *Cognitive dimension – knowledge and skills*

2. *Emotional or psychodynamic dimension – mental energy, feelings and motivations.*

3. *The social dimension – participation, communication and co-operation*
(Illeris, 2003, p 339)

Figure 3.1 Three dimensions of learning

What makes a great teacher?

Defining effective teaching is made difficult by a lack of consensus of terminology among professionals, with Coffield and Edward (2009) noting varying terms including, *good, best* or *effective* teaching. The view of effective teaching may differ according to the nature of the interested parties. An educational provider or organisation, whether they are in compulsory (primary and secondary education) or post-compulsory (further) education, will be heavily driven by external factors and outcomes (Coffield and Williamson, 2012; Perryman et al., 2011). External factors will include funding, government policy and focus and the need to meet the expectations of regulatory bodies. Outcomes for learners are traditionally seen as specific outputs in terms of qualifications and test results. Indeed, the presence of inspectorates (Ofsted in England, Estyn in Wales, Education Scotland in Scotland and the Education and Training Inspectorate in Northern Ireland) in the judgement of the quality of teaching adds further evidence to this view. However, even views of effective teaching are fluid when viewed under the omni-changing frameworks produced by inspectorates. For example, while Ofsted inspection reports previously suggested a focus on collaborative learning, a policy change in 2012 saw the removal of this suggestion, allowing teachers to decide the best way to teach their learners. Furthermore, Ofsted's decision to remove 'satisfactory' as a judgement grade (and to replace it with 'requires improvement' in September 2012) clearly indicated that satisfactory was no longer acceptable (Ofsted, 2012).

Effective teaching can also be considered in terms of superlatives with *inspirational teaching* being a phrase frequently found in literature (Sammons et al., 2014). Inspirational teaching can be considered as *Exciting, innovative and/or creative, involv[ing] immediate student engagement in the classroom* or having a *lasting effect on student aspirations and self-concept or interest in a particular subject* (Sammons et al., 2014, p 4).

Activity

In what way does this definition of inspirational teaching conflict with the expectations of inspectorates?

A key focus of inspectorates is the outcomes for learners (Ofsted, 2015b, 2015c), whereas the benefits that Sammons et al. (2014) note for learners are unmeasured outcomes of learning.

Activity

Why is it important to consider unmeasured outcomes of learning?

Confidence, interest and motivation all link to future progression and development of an individual. Therefore, while there may not be an immediate, measurable impact of learning on each of these, the longer-term impact can be significant; for example, engagement in education at a higher level or subsequent employment.

In contrast to the notions of innovation and engagement noted by Sammons et al. (2014), McBer (2000) had previously noted just three characteristics of effective teachers, those of teaching skills, professional characteristics and a positive learning environment, further evidencing the difficulty in providing a definitive view of what constitutes effective teaching. Coe et al. (2014) consider *great teaching* and suggest that great, rather than inspirational, teaching is determined by government policy. They suggest that this notion of great teaching can be narrowed to six components as noted in Table 3.1.

Table 3.1 Six components of great teaching (Coe et al., 2014)

1. Pedagogical content knowledge	Both the subject knowledge and the application of that subject knowledge.
2. Quality of instruction	Application of practical teaching skills including questioning and assessment.
3. Classroom climate	The way in which teachers engage learners, including motivation.
4. Classroom management	Effective use of the classroom and resources in addition to behaviour management.
5. Teacher beliefs	Teachers' own theories about what does and doesn't work in teaching.
6. Professional behaviours	Includes professional development, self-evaluation and reflection.

While Coe et al. recognise that *great teaching* has six components, they note that only pedagogical content knowledge and quality of instruction have strong evidence of impact on student outcomes (Coe et al., 2014). This view, however, perpetuates the view that teacher effectiveness can be judged solely on short-term student outcomes, rather than longer-term impact.

Activity

Why do you think that pedagogical content knowledge and quality of instruction are particularly influential in improving student outcomes?

Both pedagogical content knowledge and quality of instruction are clearly focused on delivery and understanding of subject matter. Therefore, if teacher effectiveness is to be measured by student outcomes, it is knowledge and application of subject matter that is measured.

The extent to which different sectors and stages of education meet the needs of pupils and learners continues to be of interest to policy-makers. Ofsted commissioned a survey into the effectiveness of Key Stage 3 and in particular the extent to which it provided pupils with *sufficient breadth and challenge, and helping them to make the best possible start to their secondary education* (Ofsted, 2015d, p 9). It raised concerns that modern foreign languages, history and geography did not lead to good levels of achievement. The report also raised concerns about behaviour in the form of low-level disrupters and the lack of challenge and engagement for learners.

Activity

Why do you think that low-level disrupters are an area of concern?

Low-level disrupters are behaviours that some teachers may choose to ignore, such as chatting, arriving late, arriving unprepared or fidgeting. They may cause learners to be distracted, not pay attention or not engage fully with a lesson.

PERSONALISED LEARNING

The level of challenge and engagement continues to be a focus in education and is noted by Coffey (2011), who emphasises the importance of differentiation. He considers differentiation as an umbrella term for a range of strategies that support individual learners. This *pedagogy of personalised learning* (DCSF, 2008, p 6) is suggested as a key focus in relation to school improvement and is multifaceted, comprising nine features, of which *High Quality Teaching and Learning* is just one. The focus of this pedagogy is learner achievement, with high expectations of learners to *reach or exceed national targets* (DCSF, 2008, p 6).

---

o *Supporting children's wider needs*

o *High quality teaching and learning*

o *Target setting and tracking*

o *Focused assessment*

o *Intervention*

o *Pupil grouping*

o *The learning environment*

o *Curriculum organisation*

o *The extended curriculum*

DCSF (2008, p 7)

Figure 3.2 Pedagogy of personalised learning: key features

Personalised learning challenges traditional teaching approaches. Rather than a teacher spreading themselves thinly, personalised learning approaches aim to overcome this and include the use of *guided work [to provide]... an alternative approach and a fair distribution of time for all children* (DCSF, 2008, p 10).

The focus on personalised learning also heralded the introduction of Quality First Teaching (QFT) – teaching of the highest quality from the outset. QFT sets out the expectations of teachers in areas ranging from lesson design, engagement through to independence and differentiation:

○ *Highly focused lesson design with sharp objectives;*

○ *High demands of pupil involvement and engagement with their learning;*

○ *High levels of interaction for all pupils;*

○ *Appropriate use of teacher questioning, modelling and explaining;*

○ *An emphasis on learning through dialogue, with regular opportunities for pupils to talk both individually and in groups;*

○ *An expectation that pupils will accept responsibility for their own learning and work*

○ *Regular use of encouragement and authentic praise to engage and motivate pupils.*

(DCSF, 2008, p 12)

Figure 3.3 Features of Quality First Teaching

Despite these recommendations, the *Education Excellence Everywhere* White Paper notes a commitment from policy-makers to encourage and support teachers and leaders to develop the best possible solutions for their pupils (DfE, 2016b).

PLANNING AND PREPARATION

At the heart of the focus on QFT noted by the DCSF (2008) is effective planning. As Lockyer (2016) comments, when done well, lesson planning can make teaching easier. It forms the bedrock of effective teaching in any classroom (Savage, 2014). However, the Independent Teacher Workload Review Group (2016, p 5) note that incorrectly perceived Ofsted requirements have led to the expectation by school leaders that teachers create *detailed plans [which] can become a 'box-ticking' exercise and create unnecessary workload for teachers.*

Activity

Why do you think that the misunderstanding over the need for detailed lesson plans may have arisen?

The most likely reason for the misunderstanding is confusion between lesson plans and planning. A good lesson will be well planned and should be supported with a planning document; however, the lesson should stand for itself rather than requiring complex and unnecessary documentation.

CORE SKILLS AND SPECIALISMS

The ever-changing focus in education is not only in relation to teaching, learning and assessment approaches, but is also linked to subject and skills specialisms. This focus, rather than being on the 'how', moves to consider the 'what' of education.

Mathematics and English/literacy

The subject focus for young people in education has, in part, returned to core subjects. Changes to government policy in England have meant that learners aged 16 who don't achieve a good pass in GCSE in maths and English will be supported and mandated to work towards and achieve this (DfBIS, 2014). This maths and English/literacy focus spans all areas of education, from primary through to secondary and post-compulsory education and training. One of the key areas noted as impacting on success in maths – that of maths anxiety – is also noted by the Scottish government who draw on OECD data *that some 30% of Scottish learners reported that they feel very tense and nervous when doing maths work and more than 50% worry that maths will be difficult* (Gov.Scot, 2016).

The importance of maths is further supported by Cymru.gov (2015) who cite Robert Lloyd Griffiths, Director of the Institute of Directors Wales, in supporting reform of the Welsh curriculum:

> *Numeracy is more important than ever in today's corporate world and the reform to the maths curriculum will equip our young people with the skills they need to meet the challenges they will come across in the modern workplace.*
>
> Cymru.gov (2015)

The results-driven reform followed the country's performance in OECD PISA tests in 2009, where mathematics was noted as a key area for development. The development need was further cemented by the PISA results of 2015, in which performance of Welsh students was below those for, England, Scotland and Northern Ireland.

This focus on maths and English/literacy achievement is of particular importance to the prospects of children and young people from disadvantaged backgrounds (see Chapter 5). As the Social Mobility and Child Poverty Commission note:

> *Young people who end up not in employment, education or training (NEET) are also predominantly those who did not do well at school – eight out of ten 16–24 year olds who are NEET left school without five good GCSEs.*
>
> (Social Mobility and Child Poverty Commission, 2014, p 1)

However, government policy in England has also moved beyond merely requiring a good pass at GCSE and has also implemented further support for maths at level 3 for students who are not studying maths at A level. This Core Maths scheme, in which maths is taught alongside technical and wider qualification further evidences the focus for young people aged 16 plus (DfE, 2015). The focus on maths will not be without additional expense. Additional funding will be required to recruit high-quality teachers to support learner progression and this is noted within the *Education Excellence Everywhere* White Paper (DfE, 2016b) in which the government recognises the impact its increased expectation will have on numbers of teachers required in shortage areas.

Vocationalism

The renewed focus on maths and English/literacy across compulsory and post-compulsory sectors has been combined with a greater move towards vocationalism. Vocationalism, a drive to overcome UK skills gaps to meet the needs of society, is evidenced in the Richards Review (2012) and the Wolf Report (2011). Michael Gove presents the Wolf Report as a *ground-breaking report* (in Wolf, 2011, p 4) and notes that *between a quarter and a third of young people between ages 16–19 are… doing nothing at all or pursuing courses which offer no route to higher levels of education or the prospect of meaningful employment* (2011, p 4). The Wolf Report recommends that to overcome this, a broader education is required between the ages of 14–19 to *avoid premature specialism.*

The move towards greater vocationalism also heralds a renewed recognition for the combined role of the workplace and education in ensuring the employability of young people. Purposeful application of apprenticeships is emphasised by the Richards Review (2012), which supports this growth of vocational training in the form of apprenticeships. Apprenticeships should be focused to *those new to a job or a role that requires sustained and substantial training.* Ofsted, however, suggested problems with apprenticeships in their 2015 survey report *Apprenticeships: Developing Skills for Future Prosperity*; they note that purposeful apprenticeships are not yet commonplace, commenting that *Some learners on low-level, low-quality programmes were unaware that they were even on an apprenticeship* (Ofsted, 2015e, p 4). Ofsted further express concerns that their inspectors have *seen too much weak provision that undermines the value of apprenticeships, especially in the service sectors and for learners aged 25 and over* (2015e, p 4). The continued focus on apprenticeships is further evidenced by the English government with a renewed commitment to require larger employers (with a wages bill over £3 million per year) to invest in apprenticeships via an apprenticeship levy (DfE, 2017b).

Activity

Explore the extent to which apprenticeship policy differs between England, Wales, Scotland and Northern Ireland.

ASSESSMENT

Muijs and Reynolds comment that *assessment is probably one of the most important but also most contentious activities teachers engage in* (2005, p 230). Assessments – whether ongoing (formative) or summative – are essential elements of teaching; however, contention arises from the fact that assessment, and in particular the use of assessment results and data, has extended beyond the classroom as a consequence of national and international policy.

Assessment and accountability

Recent years have seen a flurry of new policy in relation to all stages of education and this has led to a united reaction from educational professionals, culminating in the 2017 report by the Assessment Review Group. In this report, the group recognises that *assessment is at the heart of high quality teaching and learning*; however, it insists that *a fundamental review of statutory assessment is needed* (2017, p 2). It suggests that the fundamental purpose of assessment has been lost to *high stakes assessment*. Rather, it suggests that assessment should return to its original purpose and note six guiding principles of assessment:

---

1. *Assessment is at the core of good teaching and learning*

2. *Statutory assessment should be separated from ongoing assessment that happens in the classroom*

3. *Data from statutory assessment will never tell you the whole story of school effectiveness*

4. *The statutory assessment system should be accessible to pupils of all abilities and recognise their progress*

5. *Progress should be valued over attainment in statutory assessment*

6. *The number of statutory assessments in the primary phase should be minimised*

(Assessment Review Group, 2017, pp 6–10)

Figure 3.4 Six guiding principles of assessment

The extent to which these guiding principles of assessment are represented in government policy is conflicting. While new measures of school effectiveness do take into account prior starting points, they are still dependent on statutory assessment results.

Activity

Why do you think that statutory assessment will never tell the whole story of school effectiveness?

Statutory assessment is high-risk assessment and usually involves a decision of quality based on a single assessment point. Several factors could therefore influence the outcome of statutory assessment. Some people do not perform well in tests and exams but may be equally able as a peer who may thrive in such situations. Learners may be unwell or have other personal factors that may influence their performance on a specific day or instance.

The impact of high stakes testing was explored by Hutchings who commented that *the experiences and concerns of children and young people are shocking and sometimes upsetting* (2015, p 2). She further noted negative effects as noted in Figure 3.5.

o   *Reduction in the quality of teacher–pupil interaction*

o   *Loss of flexibility and a lack of time for teachers to respond to children as individuals*

o   *Growing pressure on children to do things before they are ready;*

o   *Focus on a narrower range of subjects.*

(Hutchings, 2015, p 2)

Figure 3.5 Negative consequences of high stakes assessment

Assessment for learning

While statutory and summative assessment plays a key role within education, ongoing formative assessment undertaken by teachers and educational professionals forms a key part of professional practice. Formative assessment and marking have developed to be a key part of a teacher's professional role, to effectively check and support learning. Assessment for Learning or AfL, an approach to assessment feedback that focused on meaningful feedback rather than grades and scores (Black et al., 2001), has been a highly influential approach in schools and colleges over recent years. Florez and Sammons (2013, p 2) state that for AfL to be used effectively it requires certain measures to be in place including supportive peer observation, discussions between teachers about learning and time allowances that enable teachers *to mark less, but mark better*. However, the Marking Policy Review Group (2016, p 6), while noting the importance of deep marking where appropriate, suggests that the original message has been *distorted*. They suggest that *providing written feedback on pupils' work – has become disproportionately valued by schools and has become unnecessarily burdensome for teachers* (2016, p 4). They attribute this in part to a desire by senior leaders to meet perceived Ofsted expectations following such methods being commended in published Ofsted reports. They further suggest that feedback to learners *can often be achieved without extensive written dialogue or comments* (2016, p 4).

Assessment continues to not only be more rigorous and challenging but its use is also expanding. This is evidenced by the introduction of times tables tests for 11-year-olds as announced by the former Secretary of State for Education Nicky Morgan. In introducing these further tests, she suggests that by identifying students that do not have these essential skills, they may be targeted in order to support their achievement (DfE, 2017a).

SUMMARY OF KEY POINTS

○ This chapter has developed your understanding of contemporary research and theories in relation to teaching, learning and assessment.

○ It has provided you with an overview of current policy direction and underpinning ideology in framing academic and vocational learning strategies.

○ It has also critically reviewed the growing importance placed on maths and English within the curriculum.

 Check your understanding

1 What educational background do young people who end up not in education, employment and training (NEET) predominantly have?

2 What is vocationalism and why is it considered important within current education policy?

3 What is Assessment for Learning (AfL) and why is it important for learners?

4 How do the components of effective teaching suggested by Coe et al. differ from those suggested by McBer?

 TAKING IT FURTHER

Illeris, K (2009) *Contemporary Theories of Learning*. Oxon: Routledge. Provides an overview of a range of contemporary and influential theories of learning.

Independent Teacher Workload Review group (2016) *Eliminating Unnecessary Workload Around Planning and Teaching Resources*. London: HMSO. Explores best practice in relation to planning and teaching resources.

Stanley, G, MacCan, R, Gardner, J, Reynolds, L and Wild, I (2009) *Review of Teacher Assessment: Evidence of What Works Best and Issues for Development*. Carrickfergus: QCA. Examines teacher assessment in a number of countries and the implication for assessing pupils' progress (APP).

REFERENCES

Assessment Review Group (2017) *Redressing the Balance*. West Sussex: NAHT.

Baird, J, Béguin, A, Black, P, Pollitt, A and Stanley, G (2011) *The Reliability Programme: Final Report of the Technical Advisory Group*. Coventry: Ofqual.

Baird, J, Johnson, S, Hopfenbeck, TN, Isaacs, T, Sprague, T, Stobart, G and Yu, G (2016) On the Supranational Spell of PISA in Policy. *Educational Research*, 58(2): 121–38.

Black. P and Wiliam, D (2001) *Inside the Black Box: Raising Standards Through Classroom Assessment*. London: GL Assessment Limited.

Bloom, BS, Engelhart, MD, Furst, EJ, Hill, WH and Krathwohl, DR (1956) *Taxonomy of Educational Objectives: The Classification of Educational Goals. Handbook I: Cognitive Domain*. New York: David McKay Company.

Coe, R, Aloisi, C, Higgins, S and Major, LE (2014) *What Makes Great Teaching? Review of the Underpinning Research*. Sutton Trust. [Online]. Retrieved from www.suttontrust.com/ researcharchive/great-teaching (accessed 23 April 2017).

Coffey, S (2011) Differentiation in Theory and Practice, in Dillon, J and Maguire, M (eds) *Becoming a Teacher: Issues in Secondary Education*. Maidenhead: Open University.

Coffield, F and Edward, S (2009) Rolling Out 'Good', 'Best' and 'Excellent' Practice. What Next? Perfect Practice? *British Educational Research Journal*, 35(3): 371–90.

Coffield, F and Williamson, B (2012) *From Exam Factories to Communities of Discovery: The Democratic Route*. London: Institute of Education.

Cymru.gov (2008) *Understanding the New Qualifications in Wales Parent Pack*. [Online]. Retrieved from: www.qualifiedforlife.org.uk (accessed 23 April 2017).

DCSF (2008) *Personalised Learning: A Practical Guide*. Nottingham: DCSF Publications.

DfBIS (2014) *The Government's Strategy to Support Workforce Excellence in Further Education*. London, HMSO.

DfE (2015) *Core Maths Qualifications: Technical Guidance*. London: HMSO.

DfE (2016a) *Progress 8 and Attainment 8: A Guide for Maintained Secondary Schools, Academies and Free Schools*. London: HMSO.

DfE (2016b) *Education Excellence Everywhere*. London: HMSO.

DfE (2017a) *Every 11-Year-Old Child to Know Times Tables by Heart*. [Online]. Retrieved from: www.gov.uk/government/news/every-11-year-old-child-to-know-times-tables-by-heart (accessed 23 April 2017).

DfE (2017b) *Guidance: Apprenticeship Funding: How it Will Work*. London: DfE. [Online]. Retrieved from: www.gov.uk/government/publications/apprenticeship-levy-how-it-will-work/apprenticeship-levy-how-it-will-work (accessed 23 April 2017).

Florez, MT and Sammons, P (2013) *Assessment for Learning: Effects and Impact*. Reading: CfBT Education Trust.

Gibb, N (2015) How E.D. Hirsch Came to Shape UK Government Policy, in Simons, J and Porter, N (eds) *Knowledge and the Curriculum: A Collection of Essays to Accompany E.D. Hirsch's Lecture at Policy Exchange*. London: Policy Exchange.

Gov.Scot (2016) *Improving Confidence and Fluency in Maths for Children, Young People, Parents and All Those Who Deliver Maths Education*. [Online] Retrieved from: www.gov.scot/Publications/2016/09/3014/4 (accessed 23 April 2017).

Hutchings, M (2015) *Exam Factories: The Impact of Accountability Measures on Children and Young People*. London: National Union of Teachers.

Illeris, K (2003) Towards a Contemporary and Comprehensive Theory of Learning. *International Journal of Lifelong Education*, 22(4): 396–406.

Illeris, K (2009) *Contemporary Theories of Learning*. Oxon: Routledge.

Independent (2013) *Letters: Gove will Bury Pupils in Facts and Rules*. [Online] Retrieved from: www.independent.co.uk/voices/letters/letters-gove-will-bury-pupils-in-facts-and-rules-8540741.html (accessed 23 April 2017).

Independent Teacher Workload Review Group (2016) *Eliminating Unnecessary Workload around Marking*. London: HMSO.

Lockyer, S (2016) *Lesson Planning for Primary School Teachers*. London: Bloomsbury.

Marking Policy Review Group (2016) *Eliminating Unnecessary Workload around Marking*. [Online]. Retrieved from: www.gov.uk/government/publications/reducing-teacher-workload-marking-policy-review-group-report (accessed 23 April 2017).

McBer, H (2000) Research into Teacher Effectiveness: A Model of Teacher Effectiveness. London: Department for Education and Employment.

Muijs, D and Reynolds, D (2005) *Effective Teaching: Evidence and Practice*, 2nd edition. London: Sage.

OECD (2017) *The Welsh Education Reform Journey*. [Online]. Retrieved from: www.oecd.org/edu/The-Welsh-Education-Reform-Journey.pdf (accessed 23 April 2017).

Ofsted (2012) *Ofsted Scraps 'Satisfactory' Judgement to Help Improve Education*. [Online]. Retrieved from www.gov.uk/government/news/ofsted-scraps-satisfactory-judgement-to-help-improve-education (accessed 23 April 2017).

Ofsted (2015a) *Initial Teacher Education Inspection Handbook*. [Online]. Retrieved from www.gov.uk/government/publications/initial-teacher-education-inspection-handbook (accessed 23 April 2017).

Ofsted (2015b) *School Inspection Handbook*. [Online]. Retrieved from www.ofsted.gov.uk/resources/school-inspection-handbook (accessed 23 April 2017).

Ofsted (2015c) *The Common Inspection Framework: Education, Skills and Early Years*. [Online]. Retrieved from www.gov.uk/government/uploads/system/uploads/attachment_data/file/461767/The_common_inspection_framework_education_skills_and_early_years.pdf (accessed 23 April 2017).

Ofsted (2015d) *Key Stage 3: The Wasted Years*. [Online]. Retrieved from www.gov.uk/government/uploads/system/uploads/attachment_data/file/459830/Key_Stage_3_the_wasted_years.pdf (accessed 23 April 2017).

Ofsted (2015e) *Apprenticeships: Developing Skills for Future Prosperity*. [Online]. Retrieved from: www.gov.uk/government/publications/apprenticeships-developing-skills-for-future-prosperity (accessed 23 April 2017).

Perryman, J, Ball, S, Maguire, M and Braun, A (2011). Life in the Pressure Cooker: School League Tables and English and Mathematics Teachers' Responses to Accountability in a Results-Driven Era. *British Journal of Educational Studies,* 59(2): 179–95.

Richards, D (2012) *The Richards Review of Apprenticeships*. London: DfE.

Sammons, P, Kington, A, Lindorff-vijayendran, A, Ortega, L and Riggall, A (2014) *Inspiring Teachers: Perspectives and Practices Summary Report*. Berkshire: CfBT Education Trust.

Savage, J (2014) *Lesson Planning: Key Concepts and Skills for Teachers*. Oxon: Routledge.

Social Mobility and Child Poverty Commission (2014) *Cracking the Code: How Schools Can Improve Social Mobility*. London: HMSO.

Wolf, A (2011) *Review of Vocational Education: The Wolf Report*. London: DfE.

Young, M (2015) What is Learning and Why Does it Matter? *European Journal of Education*, 50(1): 17–20.

081504

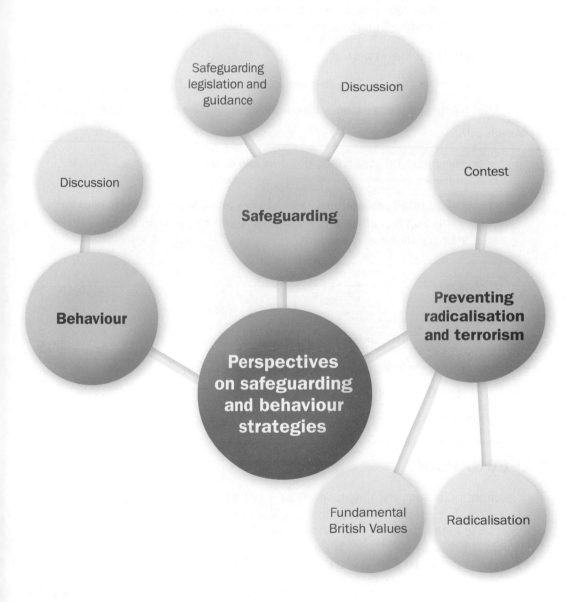

INTRODUCTION

This chapter covers two important areas of education that have continued to have prominence in government policy and guidance and feature in school inspections: safeguarding, paying particular attention to the current anti-radicalisation focus and behaviour. This chapter examines key changes and developments in both areas.

SUBJECT EXPERTISE LINKS

This chapter helps you work towards the following QAA (2015) *Subject Benchmark Statement: Education Studies* standards.

Knowledge and understanding

○ The underlying values, theories and concepts relevant to education.

○ The diversity of learners and the complexities of the education process.

Application

○ Analyse educational concepts, theories and issues of policy in a systematic way.

○ Identify and reflect on potential connections and discontinuities between each of the aspects of subject knowledge and their application in educational policies and contexts.

OBJECTIVES

The chapter develops your understanding of:

○ developments in safeguarding legislation and guidance;

○ the development of the Prevent Strategy;

○ developments in behaviour and classroom management strategies.

SAFEGUARDING

This section focuses on the development of legislation and guidance and their underlying rationale. Information about practical aspects of safeguarding and child protection can be found in the 'Taking it further' section.

Safeguarding legislation and guidance

Over the years, legislation and guidance has tended to be introduced reactively, following shortfalls in the system. For example, the Children Act (1948) was introduced following a death at the hands of foster parents and similarly, Maria Cowell's death in

1973 led to the introduction of Area Child Protection Committees (ACPCs). The ACPCs were the beginning of a more joined-up approach, coordinating the different agencies involved and later evolved into Local Safeguarding Children's Boards (LSCB), introduced under the Children Act (2004). This legislation originally specified the organisations and individuals who needed to be represented at LSCBs but recent developments will allow a more flexible response to meet the local need (Department for Education (DfE, 2016c).

Children Act (1989)

This represented one of the biggest overhauls in recent years and still influences safeguarding today in England and Wales. Significantly, this introduced key duties for local authorities:

o provide *services for children in need, their families and others* (Section 17);

o investigate *if they have reasonable cause to suspect that a child who lives, or is found, in their area is suffering, or is likely to suffer, significant harm* (Section 47).

These sections are still applied in relation to the additional support considerations, protection, or removal decisions of children.

Working Together to Safeguard Children

The Working Together to Safeguard Children guidance in its current format has been around since 1999, setting out guidance for multi-agency cooperation and is updated regularly as need dictates (HM Government, 2015a).

Children Act 2004

The introduction of the Children Act 2004 was influenced by the death of Victoria Climbié in 2000 following identification of multiple failings by a range of agencies, concluding that her death could have been avoided had a more joined-up interprofessional approach been in operation.

Safeguarding Vulnerable Groups Act (2006)

Although checks were already in place for people working with children, this Act tightened up the process of monitoring people who could work with children. This legislation resulted from the Soham murders in 2002, where failures in the system were evident. It introduced procedures that Disclosure and Barring Services (DBS) check.

Children and Families Act (2014)

This act identifies key changes to safeguarding and child protection systems and services for children and their families. It covers areas such as special educational needs and disability (SEND), children in care and adoption, placing the child at the centre of the processes and decision-making with the aim of achieving the best outcomes.

> ## Activity
>
> Have a look at a summary of some of the infamous serious cases such as those of Victoria Climbié, Holly Wells and Jessica Chapman (Soham murders), Peter Connolly, Daniel Pelka, Keanu Williams and Hamzah Khan. What did the subsequent inquiries have to report?
>
> o   What role did or should the various agencies (e.g., education, social services and police) play?

Keeping Children Safe in Education

In 2014 the government produced this statutory guidance for England and it has been updated each year since. The document covers the key expectations for schools and colleges, including roles and responsibilities for staff (DfE, 2016b).

Information sharing

One of the continuing failures in safeguarding is around the lack of inter-agency information sharing. Advice was offered in 2008 to clarify what could and should be shared to help protect children, which has been updated in a document called *Information Sharing* (HM Government, 2015b) and is to help settings and families know how to share information.

It is important that these key documents are used together as they help to understand the complete picture of prevention and action.

Discussion

It is clear to see that from the late 1980s onwards, the government has made numerous attempts to improve safeguarding for children yet the constant updates or additions to legislation, policy and guidance indicate that problems remain. For example, the inquiry and subsequent report that followed the death of Peter Connolly in 2007 identified many of the same issues that arose after the death of Victoria Climbié in 2000. Following a serious case, the response of governments has tended to be the introduction of new policy but, in reality, changes to law or guidance are only effective if effectively implemented. Munro (2011) suggests that children's services need to be less driven by procedure and policy and instead allow professionals the opportunity to exercise their professional judgement, putting the child at the centre.

When serious cases become apparent, they attract media attention, leading to a scapegoat such as a social worker who may have played a minor role in the failure. Professional misconduct may be a part of what went wrong but there is often an overreaction by social workers in the profession and situations arise where they are more inclined to take children into care to protect themselves and to avoid facing heavy criticism (Lindon and Webb, 2016). However, social workers should not be the ones to shoulder the blame; the call for greater collective accountability between involved partners suggested by Wood (2016) seems well overdue.

What also emerges is the pressure on services, so concerns regarding the cuts to spending introduced by the previous government are of relevance, resulting in less money available for children's services (Davies and Ward, 2012), compounded by a continued commitment to cost saving by the current Conservative government. Winchester (2008) suggests that cuts made to prevention, when there is a shortage of money, tend to be a false economy and result in problems later. To promote procedural change, the current government supports greater autonomy for LSCBs (DfE, 2016a). However, Davies and Ward (2012) feel an increase in local autonomy in relation to the provision of services makes joined-up working (which is often required in cases of early intervention) so much harder. However, the recent proposal of allowing LSCBs to choose their own members (DfE, 2016a) has got to be a good thing. It must be hoped this will lead to members being selected who are right for the case in question.

PREVENTING RADICALISATION AND TERRORISM

A more recent addition to the concept of safeguarding is the area of preventing radicalisation and terrorism; people working in education roles have a legal responsibility to be aware of how to safeguard children who are vulnerable to the risks of extremism and radicalisation.

Contest

The government's approach to reducing the risk of terrorism in the UK is known as CONTEST and is split into four parts.

1 *Protect – to strengthen our protection against possible terrorist attacks.*

2 *Prepare – to mitigate the impact an attack would have.*

3 *Pursue – to stop terrorist attacks from happening.*

4 *Prevent – to stop people from being drawn into terrorism.*

(HM Government, 2011)

Under the Counter-Terrorism and Security Act (2015), additional Prevent guidance is issued in the form of *The Revised Prevent Duty for England and Wales* (HM Government, 2016). It is the Prevent aspect of CONTEST that holds the most importance as part of safeguarding in school, and implementing the Prevent duty is an expectation of all educational establishments and a requirement of compliance for Office for Standards in Education, Children's Services and Skills (Ofsted) inspections. The Prevent Strategy was first published in 2011 and has three key objectives:

1 *respond to the ideological challenge of terrorism and the threat we face from those who promote it;*

2 *prevent people from being drawn into terrorism and ensure that they are given appropriate advice and support; and*

3 *work with sectors and institutions where there are risks of radicalisation that we need to address.*

(HM Government, 2016, p 2)

Prevent

Prevent is very much aimed at the pre-crime level. The Prevent duty (HM Government, 2011) makes clear that our current threat is not just from international sources but also from British-born terrorists and must be able to deal with a range of potential threats such as Al Qaeda and far-right groups. Although the strategy could be viewed as well-intended, there has been a great deal of criticism in the press surrounding Prevent. According to a BBC journalist, Casciani (2014), the government originally appeared to have a focus on Al Qaeda-inspired extremists so money was ploughed into areas with large Muslim populations. He quotes an Iman who reported anger regarding materials sent to him for use with young people, which seemed to assume Al Qaeda *was behind every street corner, working in every mosque*. Murray (2010), a journalist for *The Telegraph*, indicated this original remit led to widespread misspending as well as alienating *just about everybody*, suggesting the Prevent Strategy was seriously flawed.

Rights Watch UK (2016), a human rights charity, suggest teachers are poorly equipped to deal with this topic. They only tend to have had a few hours training at most, yet they are considered to be at the forefront of the initiative. Rights Watch UK (2016) have also suggested that several fundamental human rights have been breached by Prevent, such as the right to privacy as children are put under pressure in school to reveal personal beliefs or inform on peers. Linked to human rights, Khaleeli (2015), writing for *The Guardian,* also suggests it leads to discrimination. She reports a case where a Muslim boy was referred under Prevent guidance for asking in a lesson about nuclear fission how a bomb was made, but suggests the reaction would have been different if a non-Muslim boy asked the same question. Although the DfE (2015) stresses the Prevent duty should not stop children in schools debating controversial subjects, Khaleeli (2015) feels it could stifle freedom of speech, itself a fundamental part of British society, as well as a key human right. She suggests Muslim children are more careful about how they openly discuss contemporary issues for fear of being referred under the Prevent duty. This is further supported by Rights Watch UK (2016), who also claim the Prevent duty is hindering free speech within classrooms and by doing so becomes counterproductive. Worse, it suggests, is that issues *relating to terrorism, religion and identity* will be discussed *outside the classroom and online where simplistic narratives are promoted and go unchallenged* (Rights Watch UK, 2016, p 4). Additionally, some Muslims, wrongly identified for the Prevent programme, have begun to question where they fit in Britain today (Cobain, 2016) and in so doing potentially making them more susceptible to radicalisation.

Radicalisation

Radicalisation is the process by which a person comes to support terrorist or extremist ideologies (HM Government, 2011). It is worth noting that extremism and terrorism are not the same thing. According to the government, extremists are active, vocal and oppose Fundamental British Values (FBVs) while the Terrorism Act (2000) states that terrorism is an action that threatens or causes severe violence to a person, damage to property or interference with communication systems. Extremists can be non-violent, but according to HM Government (2011), the boundaries between extremism and terrorism are often blurred. This in itself becomes one of the issues and Rights Watch UK (2016) suggests that holding non-violent extremist views cannot possibly predict any future participation in violent acts.

However, what is clear is that radicalisation of a person takes time, so what is needed is an understanding of why they are susceptible. The Prevent Strategy (HM Government, 2011) suggests there are several factors relating to terrorism that makes people vulnerable to radicalisation. These are:

o   young people and those from lower socio-economic groups;

o   those who lack trust in the government and see conflict between their cultural identity and being British;

o   those who experience discrimination and racial harassment as well as having a negative view of the police service.

Additionally, elements such low self-esteem, the impact of social media, peer pressure or family breakdown can be a trigger towards radicalisation.

Working with young people, whether it is in a more formal capacity such as in school or a less formal situation such as a club, there is a need to be vigilant to changes in behaviour, appearance and attitude. Radicalisers have good social skills just like groomers and usually start by befriending someone who is vulnerable, making the target feel special, but they can also coerce with bullying-style tactics (HM Government, 2011). For anyone working with young people, if there is a suspicion that this might be happening with young people then specific action is needed but a more generalised approach has been promoted known as Fundamental British Values, which was introduced as part of the Prevent Strategy.

Fundamental British Values

The active promotion of British values arose in 2014, following an attempt in several Birmingham schools to promote an exclusively Islamic ethos. The DfE (2015) suggests that promoting Fundamental British Values (FBVs) can help children and young people develop resilience to radicalisation. British values are described as:

o   democracy;

o   the rule of law;

o   individual liberty;

o   mutual respect and tolerance of those of different faiths and beliefs;

o   preventing discrimination.

The DfE (2014) suggest that FBVs can be taught as part of the spiritual, moral, social and cultural provision in the school. FBVs are intended to help prepare children for life in modern Britain and are part of the current Ofsted school inspection framework (Ofsted, 2016). However, the inclusion of FBVs has led to issues for rural schools, with schools failing inspections after being criticised for inadequately preparing children for life in Britain by being 'too English' (Paton and Hall, 2014).

From its inception, FBVs have provoked controversy, with Panjwani (2016) identifying four interrelated issues:

o   The notion of Britishness, which conjured up debate in relation to identity, race and colonisation. He quotes Tomlinson (2015) suggesting that FBVs are in fact universal human values.

o   Assumptions in relation to extremism where the government sees the road to indoctrination as a singular, rather than complex, path encompassing many facets.

o   Whether monitoring of FBVs in educational establishments has impacted on free speech.

o   Each of the values themselves are unclear and open to interpretation.

Further critique of this initiative can be found in Paton and Hall (2014), who write of a school in a mainly white area being criticised by Ofsted for having too few ethnic minority pupils; something beyond their control. Further criticisms come in the shape of the National Union of Teachers, which suggests the terminology promotes the idea of *cultural supremacism* (Espinoza, 2016).

Activity

How do you think schools could promote FBVs in a way that promotes greater inclusion, diversity and tolerance?

Activities can be held in schools that are age-appropriate in relation to FBVs. For example, different cultures and faiths can be represented in the curriculum and democracy can be supported by ensuring children have a voice in school as well as discussing the election systems of Britain in comparison to other countries and discussing human rights. To further promote an international angle, work can be done in relation to understanding migration.

Channel

If radicalisation of a young person is identified as having occurred (HM Government, 2015c) then with support they can be de-radicalised by helping them to question the ideas. This is undertaken via the Channel process, a programme designed to give help at the early stages of being drawn into terrorism and avoid their exploitation before it is too late. Local authorities should have a Channel Panel made up of members from a range of services such as police, housing and social services where referrals can be made (HM Government, 2015c). Channel, set up after the July 2005 bombings in London (Kotecha, 2016), was first trialled in 2007 and eventually rolled out across England and Wales in 2012 (HM Government, 2015c). The panel aims to make a judgement of risk and work out the best intervention technique for that individual to assist them going forward (HM Government, 2015c).

Figures for 2015 indicate almost 4,000 people were referred to Channel, an increase of nearly triple from the previous year and included a child aged nine years old (Halliday,

2016). The rise in referrals should be no great surprise as there is now a statutory duty for organisations such as schools to deal with extremism and radicalisation (Counter-Terrorism and Security Act 2015) and this has helped lead to a greater awareness.

However, there have been issues. Halliday (2016) reports a case where a Muslim child of four was nearly referred by his nursery as they thought his drawing, alongside the explanation, depicted his father making a bomb; misinterpreting the child's attempts to say cucumber as 'cooker bomb'. Similar stories of overreactions are not hard to find in the press. Safeguarding children is about action but it is also important not to jump to conclusions.

 Case study

Jordan is a 16-year-old white boy who lives in a predominantly white area of the city. He is a confident young man who comes across as 'cocky' and some of his peers are a little afraid of him. He is a huge fan of his local football team, walking to the ground on a Saturday afternoon when his team are playing. To get there, he walks through a predominantly Muslim area and thinks they will not integrate as they all seem to live here. At the matches, he meets some young men a little older than him. He connects with them online and soon comes into contact with far-right material. He 'likes' these pages and shares them, hoping to impress his new friends. At the matches, they talk of Muslim 'no go' areas in the city and that there is no distinction between extremists such as members of Daesh and he begins to be convinced. His school friends notice his Facebook profile changes as does the kinds of things he 'likes' and shares and are worried (adapted from Jisc, 2016).

Activity

What sort of things do you think could happen next?

If his friends tell someone there could be the opportunity to do something positive before it is too late. Imagine they told their teacher who would then go and discuss this with the School's Designated Safeguarding Lead (DSL) The DSL talks to Jordan but also passes this concern on, and after an assessment it is decided that he is eligible to be discussed at a Channel Panel. A social worker contacts Jordon and also discusses the issue. It turns out he is worried about getting a job when he leaves school and had heard the men discussing that the Muslims were taking all the jobs. He is encouraged to join a youth club with a good mix of young people and is helped to develop new football friendships. He is also given suitable careers guidance and help to realise the path he could take.

An awareness of Prevent and what to do is imperative for people working with children and young people, so as part of safeguarding awareness and understanding of this is needed too.

BEHAVIOUR

The area of safeguarding and behaviour overlaps in the form of corporal punishment. Corporal punishment was used in schools as a way of instilling order in the classroom but this began to be seen as unacceptable and was outlawed in 1986 in English and Welsh state schools (Education (No. 2) Act). Private schools followed later in 1998 (School Standards and Framework Act). This obviously caused great debate, as corporal punishment as a sanction had been an integral aspect of school discipline, with widespread concern that this would lead to a breakdown in school discipline (Gould, 2007).

By 1988, discipline in schools was seen to be such an issue that the government asked Lord Elton to lead an enquiry triggered by concerns facing the teaching profession and how best to secure an environment conducive to teaching and learning. The report described low-level disruption as a key issue and made 138 recommendations. Among the main messages was the need for an understanding that good behaviour was a shared responsibility from the government through to schools and parents; teachers needed assistance on how to manage their classrooms and that what and how children were taught was fundamental for motivation and hence children's behaviour (Elton, 1989). A further commission was made in 2005 under Sir Alan Steer, which recognised that the Elton report was still relevant but that changes and developments in society had led to further challenges, although low-level disruption remained problematic. It advocated working with children to help them to thrive. In a later report, Steer (2009) suggested a rise in behavioural standards in school and efforts of children and their teachers should be recognised. Again, recommendations focused around making lessons more engaging. There was widespread disagreement at the time from the Opposition to the government and from teachers suggesting that school suspensions were on the increase and that behaviour had deteriorated (MacLeod, 2009). Also in contrast to Steer, was a survey by the union, the Association of Teachers and Lecturers (ATL), that suggested disruptive behaviour was actually the norm (ATL, 2009). More recently, Haydn (2014) suggested that Ofsted was reporting improving standards of behaviour, but Haydn argued that this was due to them being presented with an inaccurate picture during inspections, a claim that is also backed up by the latest independent report by Tom Bennett (2017).

With a change of government in 2010, further advice was sought and a behavioural checklist called *Getting the Simple Things Right* was produced. It offered straightforward advice, but an overall message was about consistent implementation of behaviour policies (Taylor, 2011) and this is a common theme across much of the literature regarding behaviour. Another key piece of guidance is *Behaviour and Discipline in Schools*, first published in 2013 and last updated in 2016. This is for all schools in England and outlines best practice, including the requirement for a behaviour policy, which for maintained schools should be published on the website and academy schools are advised to do so as well (DfE, 2016a).

Discussion

The use of corporal punishment as a behavioural deterrent continues to be a topic of conversation that is visited at regular intervals and a survey commissioned by the *Times*

Educational Supplement (TES) found that nearly a half of parents alongside one-fifth of pupils feel that the use of the cane should be applied as an 'ultimate' sanction (Stewart, 2011). However, the report suggests previous research in 2008 indicated almost three-quarters of teachers were opposed to the use of such punishment, perhaps because as Gould (2007) highlights, a minority of teachers abused this power. How teachers manage classroom behaviour impacts on pupils' ability to learn, which is why it is one of the areas that Ofsted examine in the current school inspection (Ofsted, 2016), with the quality of the lessons being prominent. Behaviour retains prominence on the government's agenda; first, as Haydn (2014) outlines, behaviour in the classroom is one of the main reasons teachers cite for leaving the profession. Second, comparative studies such as the Programme for International Student Achievement (PISA) suggest that teachers in England are working in more challenging conditions than their peers in other countries, with low-level disruption common (OECD, 2015). The OECD (2015) also notes that the countries reporting limited disruption in lessons performed better in the tests. The current focus in the latest independent review, commissioned by the government, is in relation to school leadership and their responsibility to create an ethos and culture that encourages good behaviour (Bennett, 2017).

SUMMARY OF KEY POINTS

○ Safeguarding legislation and guidance is extensive and constantly being updated.

○ The Prevent duty is currently a key aspect of the government's approach to tackling radicalisation and preventing terrorism, and educational establishments have a role to play.

○ There is a legal responsibility connected with Prevent for all educators.

○ Behaviour in schools continues to promote governmental guidance and school leadership is the latest area of emphasis.

 # Check your understanding

1 What document is of particular interest if advice on multi-agency working is required?

2 What is CONTEST?

3 What is the Prevent Strategy?

4 Why would someone be referred to Channel?

5 Where would a school need to look for advice on its duties in relation to behaviour?

TAKING IT FURTHER

DfE (2015) *The Prevent Duty: Departmental Advice for Schools and Childcare Providers*. London: DfE. For the latest governmental guidelines for schools and childcare facilities.

DfE (2016a) *Behaviour and Discipline in Schools: Advice for Headteachers and School Staff*. London: DfE. For the governmental guidelines on behaviour.

DfE (2016b) *Keeping Children Safe in Education*. London: DfE. For latest governmental guidelines as to best practice.

Hall, F, Hindmarch, D, Hoy, D and Machin, L (2015) *Supporting Primary Teaching and Learning*. Northwich: Critical Publishing. For a practical look at school-based practice see Chapters 3 and 4.

HM Government (2015) *Working Together to Safeguard Children: A Guide to Inter-Agency Working to Safeguard and Promote the Welfare of Children*. London: DfE. For the latest governmental guidelines into interagency safeguarding procedures.

For information regarding safeguarding in Scotland, Wales and Northern Ireland, see www.nspcc.org.uk/preventing-abuse/child-protection-system.

For information regarding behaviour in Scotland, see www.gov.scot/Topics/Education/Schools/HLivi/behaviour.

For information regarding behaviour in Northern Ireland, see www.education-ni.gov.uk/articles/behaviour-school.

For information regarding behaviour in Wales, see http://learning.gov.wales/docs/learningwales/publications/140822-behaviour-management-handbook-for-primary-schools-en.pdf.

REFERENCES

ATL (2009) *Primary School Behaviour Survey*. London: ATL. [Online]. Retrieved from: www.atl.org.uk/Images/ATL%20primary%20school%20behaviour%20survey.pdf (accessed 23 April 2017).

Bennett, T (2017) *Creating a Culture: How School Leaders Can Optimise Behaviour*. London: Department for Education.

Casciani, D (2014) *Analysis: The Prevent Strategy and its Problems.* [Online]. Retrieved from: www.bbc.co.uk/news/uk-28939555 (accessed 23 April 2017).

Cobain, I (2016) *UK's Prevent Counter-Radicalisation Policy 'Badly Flawed'*. [Online]. Retrieved from: www.theguardian.com/uk-news/2016/oct/19/uks-prevent-counter-radicalisation-policy-badly-flawed (accessed 23 April 2017).

Davies, C and Ward, H (2012) *Safeguarding Children Across Services: Messages from Research*. London: Jessica Kingsley Publishers.

DfE (2014) *Promoting British Values as Part of SMSC in Schools*. London: DfE.

DfE (2015) *The Prevent Duty Departmental Advice for Schools and Childcare Providers*. London: DfE.

DfE (2016a) *Behaviour and Discipline in Schools: Advice for Headteachers and School Staff*. London: DfE.

DfE (2016b) *Keeping Children Safe in Education: Statutory Guidance for Schools and Colleges*. London: DfE.

DfE (2016c) *Review of the Role and Functions of Local Safeguarding Children Boards: The Government's Response to Alan Wood CBE*. London: DfE.

Elton, R (1989) *Behaviour and Discipline in Schools*. London: Her Majesty's Stationary Office.

Espinoza, J (2016) *Teaching Children Fundamental British Values Is an Act of 'Cultural Supremacism'*. [Online]. Retrieved from: www. telegraph.com/news/2016/03/28/ teaching-children-fundamental-british-values-is-act-of-cultural (accessed 23 April 2017).

Gould, M (2007) *Sparing the Rod*. [Online]. Retrieved from: www.theguardian.com/ education/2007/jan/09/schools.uk1 (accessed 23 April 2017).

Hall, F, Hindmarch, D, Hoy, D and Machin, L (2015) *Supporting Primary Teaching and Learning*. Northwich: Critical Publishing.

Halliday, J (2016) *Almost 4,000 People Referred to UK Deradicalisation Scheme Last Year*. [Online]. Retrieved from: www.theguardian.com/uk-news/2016/mar/20/almost-4000-people-were-referred-to-uk-deradicalisation-scheme-channel-last-year (accessed 23 April 2017).

Haydn, T (2014) To What Extent Is Behaviour a Problem in English Schools? Exploring the Scale and Prevalence of Deficits in Classroom Climate. *Review of Education,* 2(1): 31–64.

HM Government (2011) *Prevent Strategy*. Norwich: TSO.

HM Government (2015a) *Working Together to Safeguard Children. A Guide to Inter-Agency Working to Safeguard and Promote the Welfare of Children*. London: DfE.

HM Government (2015b) *Information Sharing*. London: DfE.

HM Government (2015c) *Channel Duty Guidance Protecting Vulnerable People from Being Drawn into Terrorism: Statutory Guidance for Channel Panel Members and Partners of Local Panels*. London: Home Office.

HM Government (2016) *The Revised Prevent Duty for England and Wales*. London: HM Government.

Jisc (2016) *Workshop to Raise Awareness of Prevent (WRAP)*. [Online]. Retrieved from: www. jisc.ac.uk/advice/training/workshop-to-raise-awareness-of-prevent-wrap (accessed 23 April 2017).

Khaleeli, H (2015) *'You Worry They Could Take Your Kids': Is The Prevent Strategy Demonising Muslim Schoolchildren?* [Online]. Retrieved from: www.theguardian.com/ uk-news/2015/sep/23/prevent-counter-terrorism-strategy-schools-demonising-muslim-children (accessed 23 April 2017).

Kotecha, S (2016) *More Than 400 Children Under 10 Referred for 'Deradicalisation'*. Retrieved from: www.bbc.co.uk/news/uk-35360375 (accessed 23 April 2017).

Lindon, J and Webb, J (2016) *Safeguarding Children and Child Protection*, 5th edition. London: Hodder Education.

MacLeod, D (2009) *Behaviour in Schools is Improving, Says Sir Alan Steer. Who Believes Him?* [Online]. Retrieved from: www.theguardian.com/education/mortarboard/2009/apr/15/steer-behaviour-report (accessed 23 April 2017).

Munro, E (2011) *Munro Review of Child Protection: Final Report – a Child-Centred System.* London: TSO.

Murray, D (2010) *The Prevent Strategy: A Textbook Example of How to Alienate Just About Everybody.* [Online]. Retrieved from:www.thetelegrah.co.uk/news/uknews/terrorism-in-the-uk/7540456/The-Prevent-strategy-a-textbook-example-of-how-to-alienate-just-about-everybody.html (accessed 23 April 2017).

OECD (2015) *PISA 2015 Results: Policies and Practices for Successful Schools Volume II.* Paris: OECD Publishing. [Online]. Retrieved from: www.keepeek.com/Digital-Asset-Management/oecd/education/pisa-2015-results-volume-ii_9789264267510-en#page1 (accessed 23 April 2017).

Ofsted (2016) *The Common Inspection Framework: Education, Skills and Early Years.* Manchester: Ofsted.

Panjwani, F (2016) Towards an Overlapping Consensus: Muslim Teachers' Views on Fundamental British Values. *Journal of Education for Teaching*, 42(3): 329–40.

Paton, G and Hall, M (2014) *Ofsted: Rural Schools 'Failing to Promote British Values'.* [Online]. Retrieved from: www.telegraph.co.uk/education/educationnews/11253436/Ofsted-rural-schools-failing-to-promote-British-values.html (accessed 23 April 2017).

Rights Watch UK (2016) *Preventing Education: Human Rights and UK Counter Terrorism Policy in Schools.* London: Rights Watch UK.

Steer, A (2005) *Learning Behaviour: The Report of the Practitioners Group on School Behaviour and Discipline.* Nottingham: DfES.

Steer, A (2009) *Learning Behaviour: Lessons Learned. A Review of Behaviour Standards and Practices in Our Schools.* Nottingham: DfES.

Stewart, W (2011) *Parents Dust Down the Cane.* London: TES.

Taylor, C. (2011) *Getting the Simple Things Right: Charlie Taylor's Behaviour Checklists.* London: DfE.

Tomlinson, S (2015) The Empire Disintegrates. *Ethnic and Racial Studies*, 38(13): 2208–15.

Winchester, R (2008) *Change for the Better.* [Online]. Retrieved from: www.theguardian.com/society/2008/oct/22/every-child-matters (accessed 23 April 2017).

Wood, A. (2016) *Wood Report: Review of the Role and Functions of Local Safeguarding Children Boards.* London: DfE.

Inclusion, equality and special educational needs

Equality

Bullying

Inclusion in the classroom and beyond

Inclusion, equality and special educational needs

The history of inclusion, equality and SEND

The importance of social mobility

Grammar schools

Pupil Premium

INTRODUCTION

This chapter develops your understanding of key issues in relation to educational equality: social mobility, inclusion and special educational needs and disability (SEND). To achieve this, it examines key terms, analyses historical perspectives and evaluates the effectiveness of associated education strategies.

SUBJECT EXPERTISE LINKS

This chapter helps you work towards the following QAA (2015) *Subject Benchmark Statement: Education Studies* standards.

Knowledge and understanding

o   The underlying values, theories and concepts relevant to education.

o   The diversity of learners and the complexities of the education process.

o   The societal and organisational structures and purposes of educational systems, and the possible implications for learners and the learning process.

Reflection

o   The ability to reflect on their own and others' value systems.

OBJECTIVES

This chapter develops your understanding of:

o   key terminology in relation to social mobility, inclusion, equality and SEND;

o   the history of inclusion, equality and SEND in education;

o   the importance of meeting the needs of children and young people with special educational needs and disability (SEND);

o   the importance of social mobility in ensuring equality in education and society;

o   inclusivity in the classroom and beyond.

EQUALITY

The Equality and Human Rights Commission (EHRC), the statutory body responsible for upholding the Equalities Act (2010), considers equality to be about:

Ensuring that every individual has an equal opportunity to make the most of their lives and talents, and believing that no one should have poorer life chances because of where, what or whom they were born, what they believe, or whether they have a disability.

(EHRC, 2017)

Just as in society, children and young people in education have a variety of needs that are recognised within the Equality Act (2010) and it is the responsibility of teachers and educational professionals to adhere to this legislation to support those needs. The Equality Act brought together a range of legislation in relation to discrimination and identifies nine protected characteristics: age, disability, gender reassignment, race, religion or belief, sex, sexual orientation, marriage and civil partnership, and pregnancy and maternity. However *Age and being married or in a civil partnership are NOT protected characteristics for the schools provisions* (EHRC, 2017, p 8). This amalgamation of legislation and duties had the aim of making equality *less bureaucratic and more outcome-focused* (DfE, 2014). Within education, equality is about fairness and equity. It is about giving children and young people the opportunity to succeed and in doing so should not be confused with treating them all the same. Rather, it is about recognising their differences and ensuring equality of opportunity for all by making reasonable adjustments to meet differing needs.

Activity

Why is equality not about treating learners all the same?

Equality is based around the outcomes for the learners; therefore, in order to achieve the same outcome, two learners may have quite different needs. By supporting each learner appropriately to their needs to achieve the same outcome, you are helping to ensure equality.

THE HISTORY OF INCLUSION, EQUALITY AND SEND

The origins of the incorporation of SEND within the education system, rather than as separate provision, can be traced to the Education Act (1944). Commonly known as the Butler Act, after its author, the education minister Richard 'Rab' Butler, this Act made a number of changes to education in England and Wales. It was a major milestone in social justice in education that also established the notion of secondary education for all ages (Chitty, 2009). In this seminal Act, 11 categories of disabilities were recognised, encompassing both learning and physical disabilities. The terminology used in the report, however, is far removed from language that is acceptable in modern society, demonstrating a positive shift in recent years in terms of inclusivity. Society has made significant progress away from the use of negative and highly inappropriate terms

used in the Butler Act of learners being *handicapped* or *sub-normal*. However, significant progression was not made for more than three decades, until the publication of
the Warnock Report in 1978, which led to fundamental changes to SEND provision still
relevant to the present day.

The Warnock Report (1978) made a number of groundbreaking recommendations in
terms of special educational needs in England, Scotland and Wales, but in particular, it
informed that:

> *The planning of services for children and young people should be based on the
> assumption that about one in six children at any time and up to one in five chil-
> dren at some time during their school career will require some form of special
> educational provision.*

(Warnock, 1978, p 338)

With its recognition of the widespread nature of special educational needs, the Warnock
Report was instrumental in changing the terminology and perceptions of SEND.
Commonly used vocabulary today, such as 'learning difficulties', emerged from the
report and presented such needs in a more positive and inclusive light. The Warnock
Report further introduced the specialised system of recording and building of an educational profile to document and support the needs of young people with complex and
long-term disabilities. The report also argued that children with SEND should be taught
in mainstream education, rather than in specialist schools as in the past (Chitty, 2009).
However in their third report of 2005–6, the House of Commons Educational and Skills
Committee on Special Educational Needs, building on Warnock's own criticism of SEND
provision, commented:

> *It is the view of this Committee that the original Warnock framework has run
> its course. With Ofsted identifying a 'considerable inequality of provision', the
> SEN system is demonstrably no longer fit for purpose and there is a need for the
> Government to develop a new system that puts the needs of the child at the cen-
> tre of provision.*

(House of Commons Educational and Skills Committee on
Special Educational Needs, 2006, p 10)

In an interview with the *Times Educational Supplement* (TES, 2003), Warnock suggested
that *the way schools care for children with special needs is a disastrous waste of money
and must be overhauled.* Although Barton (2005) comments on the *contentious nature
of the question of inclusive education*, while recognising the insightful historical consideration, he suggests that Warnock is guilty of *naivety, arrogance and ignorance*, suggesting that she has made *several unsubstantiated claims and assertions* while failing
to draw on the views of the disabled themselves (2005, pp 1–3).

Most recently, the 2015 SEND Code of Practice aims to provide children in England
between the ages of 0 to 25 with *a system which is less confrontational and more efficient* (DfE, 2015b, p 11). This publication, as with much government policy, is linked to
outcomes and aspirations of children and young people and in particular their *transition
to adulthood*, rather than only meeting their needs at a specific time. Furthermore, it

introduced a greater involvement of parents and children in the decision-making around their individual needs. However, the scale of the new Code of Practice means significant changes that will require close attention in order to be successfully implemented (SecEd, 2014).

The provision for Special Educational needs across the United Kingdom is reliant on legislation and codes of practice specific to the separate constituent countries. For example, the Education (Additional Support for Learning) (Scotland) Act 2004 and subsequent 2009 amendments are the key Acts in relation to meeting the needs of children and young people with SEND in Scotland. In Wales, the Additional Learning Needs and Education Tribunal (Wales) Bill is the basis of current provision for young people with Additional Learning Needs, a change in terminology from the use of SEND in England. However, in Northern Ireland, the legislation comprises the Education (Northern Ireland) Order 1996 as amended by the Special Educational Needs and Disability (Northern Ireland) Order 2005 (SENDO) and the Special Educational Needs and Disability Act (Northern Ireland) 2016. The SEND Act introduces a number of changes to SEN policy, including the need for a personal learning plan for children and young people with SEN, a requirement for cooperation between educational, health and social services organisations and a right to appeal after an annual review (Perry, 2016).

Activity

Explore the differences and similarities between the English, Scotland, Wales and Northern Ireland codes of practice and legislation for special educational needs.

Four categories of special educational need are highlighted by the Department for Education in their 2015 Code of Practice:

1   *communication and interaction;*

2   *cognition and learning;*

3   *social, emotional and mental health;*

4   *sensory and/or physical needs.*

The DfE does, however, recognise that the needs of children may not easily be classified within just one of the categories, noting that: *individual children often have needs that cut across all these areas and their needs may change over time* (2015b, p 85).

Disability can be viewed in terms of a social or medical model, whereas the medical model is based, not upon what a person needs, but rather upon fixing their impairments, the social model is based on a disability being a consequence of the structure of society and is based on removing barriers (Scope, 2017). The social model of disability is based on equality and is therefore key in creating an inclusive education system and society. Conversely the medical model is viewed by many to be divisive as it *looks at what is 'wrong' with the person, not what the person needs. It creates low expectations and leads to people losing independence, choice and control in their own lives* (Scope, 2017)

The focus of meeting the needs of children and young people with special educational needs and disabilities commences with Early Years provision and the need for this is noted within the SEN Code of Practice, which comments on the importance of avoiding any delay in providing appropriate support. Meeting special educational needs is a responsibility that is shared between a range of professionals, in areas such as health and speech and language therapists via an Educational Health Care Plan.

Norwich and Black (2015) noted that the distribution variation of secondary school-aged students with SEND was not consistent between school types in the English school system. They found lower proportions of students with SEND in converter academies (successful schools that have opted to benefit from autonomy) than in maintained schools and sponsored academies (low-performing schools who are mandated to become an academy and are supported by a sponsor). This appears to offer support for the findings by Muir and Clifton, who note concern that:

> Children with special educational needs are losing out, particularly because of the way in which some schools deploy covert selection, and because individual schools are often not best placed to commission specialist services.
>
> (Muir and Clifton, 2014, p 1)

The most recent data in relation to SEND identifies the following:

15.4% of pupils in schools in England have identified special educational needs

23.8% of pupils with a primary need were recorded as having 'Moderate Learning Difficulty' as their primary need – the most common primary need

(DfE, 2015a, p 1)

The importance of an education system with professionals who have access to suitable training to meet the needs of learners with SEND is noted within the *Educational Excellence Everywhere* White Paper (DfE, 2016). This White Paper confirms an ongoing investment, not only in supporting trainee teachers' awareness of SEND with appropriate training, but also training for existing teachers and educational professionals in order to improve outcomes for children and young people. The DfE further notes an ongoing commitment to ensuring that their policy and support of pupils with SEND is based on a stronger evidence base.

THE IMPORTANCE OF SOCIAL MOBILITY

While the Equality Act (2010) appears all-encompassing, there are additional areas of equality that are of key interest to educational professionals, although they are not enshrined in the legislation. The DfBIS (2011) notes the difficulty in defining social mobility, though suggest that it refers to *the ability of individuals from disadvantaged backgrounds to move up in the world, akin to the notion of equality of opportunity* (2011, p 6). It therefore forms an essential component of an inclusive and equitable society. Consecutive governments have expressed concern regarding the lack of social mobility evident in society. However, in a speech to the British Academy, Goldthorpe (2016) suggests that this concern has failed to transform into improved social mobility: *the historical record indicates that the effect of educational expansion and reform on mobility processes and outcomes has in fact been very limited.* Social mobility therefore, still remains a concern as noted by the Sutton Trust (2016), which comments that *low social mobility and lack of educational opportunity is arguably the biggest social challenge of our times.*

The Ofsted 2013 report *Unseen Children: Access and Achievement 20 Years On* built on findings in the *Access and Achievement in Urban Education* report that noted widespread underachievement for young people. At the heart of the report was the recognition that young people from disadvantaged backgrounds still had the potential to achieve well in education and in life. It recognised the chances for disadvantaged young people were still too low and suggested that: *a large minority of children still [did not succeed] at school or college, becoming increasingly less visible as they progress through the system* (Ofsted, 2013, p 5).

Most recently, in 2017, the All Party Parliamentary Group presented a report that recognised that young people from disadvantaged backgrounds were *less successful than their more advantaged counterparts in getting in to the top professions* (APPG, 2017, p 2). To overcome this, the group made some key recommendations based upon *a strategic approach to social mobility.* Their recommendations spanned the need to overcome *financial barriers, ensure fair and transparent recruitment practices to the professions and to ensure high quality careers advice to young people* (APPG, 2017, p 2). Additionally, the report suggested that access to the top professions required more than subject specialist skills and noted the need for development of: *resilience, confidence and self- motivation* (APPG, 2017, p 5).

One of the most important factors in supporting social mobility and breaking intergenerational disadvantage has been noted as the influence of their parents, particularly in relation to support with education (Hartas, 2014). This is supported by the Equality Trust (2017), which comments:

> *Although good school systems make a difference, the biggest influence on educational attainment is family background, so disadvantaged children do less well at school and miss out on the benefits of education.*
>
> (Equality Trust, 2017)

Richards et al. (2016) found that parental input, including homework support or involvement at parents' evenings, led to improved outcomes for learners. They further noted the perpetuation of positive attitude of the middle classes throughout society as contributing to the ongoing socio-economic gap. This, however, does not mean a lack of effort or engagement on the part of other parents. The Social Mobility Commission (2016) recognises that parents with lower educational backgrounds are spending more than twice the amount of time on educational activities than they did in the 1970s, although they note that there was not the marked difference in income that exists today.

Pupil Premium

The introduction in 2011 of Pupil Premium indicated a commitment to improving outcomes for disadvantaged children and young people. Ainscow et al. (2016, p 16) considers this attempt to: *tackle educational disadvantage through the Pupil Premium as the major contribution of the post-2010 governments' attempts to address diversity*. Pupil Premium is additional government funding for publicly funded schools and is targeted at children from low-income families, looked-after children and armed forces families. It aims to get to the heart of social disadvantage and reduce the attainment gap between those groups and their peers. Ofsted noted inconclusive evidence regarding the impact that Pupil Premium had on changing the way that schools supported pupils from disadvantaged backgrounds: *Only one in 10 [schools] said that it had significantly changed the way they work, while approximately one in six said that it had had no impact at all* (Ofsted, 2012b, p 4).

However, in his foreword to *Pupil Premium: Next Steps* (Sutton Trust, 2015, p 2) Sir Peter Lampl comments on the positive impact of Pupil Premium:

> There is no doubt that the pupil premium has enabled schools – including many in areas not traditionally seen as facing significant disadvantage – to do more to improve the results of their less advantaged pupils.
>
> (Sutton Trust, 2015, p 2)

In reviewing the impact of Pupil Premium, Ofsted blamed weak leadership and governance in schools where no impact is evident. They cite their own inspection reports in support of this and suggest that insufficient progress is due to the lack of senior leadership analysis into the performance of different groups of students and the impact of Pupil Premium funding (Ofsted, 2014).

Grammar schools

In the 2016 Autumn Statement (HM Treasury, 2016), the government evidenced a financial commitment to the growth of grammar schools to the extent of £50 million per year from 2017/18. The Conservative Prime Minister Theresa May further cemented this commitment with the goal of *decisively shifting Britain's education system and building a great meritocracy so that children from ordinary working families are given the chances their richer contemporaries take for granted* (cited in Rayner, 2017). This aim has echoes of the introduction of the tripartite system of education following the 1944 Education Act with the aim of equal opportunities for all (Forester and Garratt, 2016). However, the extent to which grammar schools can achieve this laudable aim is challenged by the Education Policy Institute (EPI) who note the absence of any overall impact on attainment. Furthermore, they note that disadvantaged pupils are underrepresented in grammar schools. The notion of selection is further drawn into this discussion, with evidence that greater selection can lead to negative outcomes. As the EPI (2016) comment: *Disadvantaged pupils who live in a wholly selective local authority but do not go to a selective school, have lower attainment than those who live in a non-selective authority*. Furthermore, the link between grammar schools and social mobility is firmly rebutted by Andrews and Hutchinson (2016, p 5) who assert that *there is no evidence that an increase in selection would have any positive impact on social mobility.*

INCLUSION IN THE CLASSROOM AND BEYOND

Whereas inclusion has traditionally been used to refer to learners with SEND within mainstream schools, inclusion and inclusivity are much wider-reaching in terms of their impact on children and young people in any learning environment. At its heart, an inclusive learning environment is one in which each and every learner is included in lessons (Huddleston and Unwin, 2013).

Bullying

Providing an inclusive learning environment may be in terms of not excluding children and young people for reasons of SEND or a protected characteristic as noted within the Equality Act (2010). However, it may also be in relation to their emotional well-being and issues of bullying also form a key part of ensuring inclusivity. Smith and Brain (2000, p 1) define bullying as *aggressive behaviour normally characterized by repetition and imbalance of power.* The consequences of bullying range from mental health problems such as anxiety and depression and in some cases self-harm and suicide. Bullying may be targeted against groups of children and young people; for example, in research undertaken in 12 Scottish schools with gypsy and show traveller students, Lloyd and Stead (2001, p 361) found that the students *experienced frequent racist bullying and name calling.* Prevention and strategies to overcome bullying are therefore a key issue in ensuring an inclusive learning environment. Smith (2014, p 5) comments that in the past, *school actions about bullying have been nonexistent, or unplanned and ineffective.* He suggests that this may in part be due to a lack of awareness of the consequences of bullying. He does, however, recognise that much has changed in recent years, not only in the terms of *the culture regarding bullying* (2014, p 185) but also the fact that schools and often pupils are actively involved in actions to prevent bullying.

Bullying is evolving with twenty-first century technology and a new aspect is emerging – that of cyberbullying. Cyberbullying is any form of bullying undertaken with electronic technology; it may be via text message, social media or even in chat rooms and requires a different approach than that used to address bullying in the past. Rivers and Noret (2010) undertook research into cyberbullying over a four-year period. In their research with Year 7 and 8 pupils in secondary schools in the north of England, they found an increase in incidences of pupils receiving *nasty or threatening text messages [although] receipt of frequent nasty or threatening text and email messages remained relatively stable* (Rivers and Noret, 2010, p 643). Nevertheless, Kowalski et al. (2012) suggest that social media may also be a key tool in challenging and preventing cyberbullying. (See Chapter 10 for further consideration of children's online rights.) Similarly, initiatives to prevent cyberbullying and bullying are increasingly being delivered by young people themselves, for example the growth of Anti-Bullying Ambassadors within schools.

While the involvement of young people is key in tackling bullying, so too is the involvement of the school. This is recognised by Ofsted (2012a): in their *No Place for Bullying* report, Ofsted clearly linked the culture and ethos of the school to positive behaviour and a reduction in bullying. They found that in a small number of schools this did not occur and therefore inter-pupil relations were inconsistent and *the culture and the curriculum did not effectively develop pupils' understanding about diversity or help them to develop sufficient empathy for each other* (Ofsted 2012a, p 5). Ofsted further recognised the wider role of school organising in tackling bullying, ranging from the structure of break times and the way in which the school was physically organised.

SUMMARY OF KEY POINTS

This chapter has explored your understanding of inclusion, equality and SEND, including recognition that:

○   Equality is about fairness and ensuring equality of opportunity for all.

○   SEND has undergone many changes from the Butler Act of 1944 to the 2015 Code of Practice, moving away from negative terminology and notions of *handicap* to a focus on inclusivity.

○   Socio-economic status is a key factor influencing outcomes for children and young people and therefore positive social mobility is a key goal of education.

○   There is a clear shift in government policy towards wider implementation of grammar schools despite evidence of no overall attainment impact and a negative impact in highly selective areas for those young people who do not go to grammar schools (EPI, 2016).

○   Bullying continues to be a key educational issue and is evolving with technology.

   Check your understanding

1   Compare definitions of inclusion, equality, SEND and social mobility from the government and relevant charities.

2   What themes can you identify in the Warnock Report and SEND Code of Practice?

3   Why is school organisation important in preventing bullying?

4   What is an inclusive learning environment?

TAKING IT FURTHER

The Diana Award's Anti-Bullying Campaign involves different projects aimed at reducing bullying in schools: www.antibullyingpro.com.

Goepel, J, Childerhouse, H and Sharpe, S (2015) *Inclusive Primary Teaching: A Critical Approach to Equality and Special Educational Needs and Disability.* Northwich: Critical Publishing. A fully updated equality and child-centred approach to inclusive teaching.

The Sutton Trust, www.suttontrust.com. The Sutton Trust are key commissioners of research into the use of education to improve social mobility.

REFERENCES

Ainscow, M, Dyson, A, Hopwood, L and Thomson, S (2016) *Primary Schools – Responding to Diversity: Barriers and Possibilities.* York: Cambridge Primary Review Trust.

Andrews, J and Hutchinson, J (2016) *Grammar Schools and Social Mobility: Further Analysis of Policy Options.* London: Education Policy Institute.

APPG (All Party Parliamentary Group) (2017) *The Class Ceiling: Increasing Access to the Leading Professions.* [Online]. Retrieved from: www.socialmobilityappg.co.uk (accessed 23 April 2017).

Barton, L (2005) *Special Educational Needs: An Alternative Look.* [Online]. Retrieved from: www.disability-studies.leeds.ac.uk/files/library/Barton-Warnock.pdf (accessed 23 April 2017).

Butler Act (1944) *The Cabinet Papers 1915–1982.* [Online]. Retrieved from www. nationalarchives.gov.uk/cabinetpapers/themes/butler-act.htm (accessed 23 April 2017).

Chitty, C (2009) *Education Policy in Britain*, 2nd edition. Basingstoke: Palgrave Macmillan.

DfBIS (2011) *Social Mobility: A Literature Review,* London: Department of Business, Innovation and Skills.

DfE (2012) Support and *Aspiration: A New Approach* to *Special Educational Needs* and *Disability – Progress* and *Next Steps.* London: HMSO.

DfE (2014) *The Equality Act 2010 and Schools: Departmental Advice for School Leaders, School Staff, Governing Bodies and Local Authorities.* London: HMSO.

DfE (2015a) *Statistical First Release: Special Educational Needs in England: January 2015.* London: HMSO.

DfE (2015b) *Special Educational Needs and Disability Code of Practice: 0 to 25 Years – Statutory Guidance for Organisations Which Work with and Support Children and Young People who have Special Educational Needs or Disabilities.* London: HMSO.

DfE (2016) *Educational Excellence Everywhere.* London: HMSO.

EHRC (2017) *Understanding Equality – What is Equality?* [Online]. Retrieved from www.equalityhumanrights.com/en/secondary-education-resources/useful-information/understanding-equality (accessed 23 April 2017).

EPI (2016) *Grammar Schools: 8 Conclusions from the Data.* [Online]. Retrieved from: https://epi.org.uk/analysis/grammar-schools-8-conclusions-data (accessed 23 April 2017).

Equality Trust (2017) *Education – Children Do better in Equal Societies.* [Online]. Retrieved from: www.equalitytrust.org.uk/education (accessed 23 April 2017).

Forrester, G and Garratt, D (2016) *Education Policy Unravelled*, 2nd edition. London: Bloomsbury.

Goldthorpe, J (2016) *Social Class Mobility in Modern Britain: Changing Structure, Constant Process.* [Online]. Retrieved from: www.britac.ac.uk/events/social-class-mobility-modern-britain-changing-structure-constant-process (accessed 23 April 2017).

Hartas, D (2014) Parenting for Social Mobility? Home Learning, Parental Warmth, Class and Educational Outcomes. *Journal of Education Policy*, 30(1): 21–38.

HM Treasury (2016) *Autumn Statement 2106.* [Online]. Retrieved from www.gov.uk/government/publications/autumn-statement-2016-documents/autumn-statement-2016#executive-summary (accessed 23 April 2017).

Huddleston, P and Unwin, L (2013) *Teaching and Learning in Further Education: Diversity and Change*, 4th edition. Abingdon: Routledge.

Kowalski, RM, Limber, SP and Agatston, P (2012) *Cyber Bullying: Bullying in the Digital Age.* Chichester: John Wiley and Sons.

Lloyd, G and Stead, J (2001) 'The Boys and Girls Not Calling Me Names and the Teachers to Believe Me': Name Calling and the Experiences of Travellers in School. *Children and Society*, 15: 361–74.

Muir, R and Clifton, J (2014) *Whole System Reform: England's Schools and the Middle Tier.* London: IPPR.

Norwich, B and Black, A (2015) The Placement of Secondary School Students with Statements of Special Educational Needs in the More Diversified System of English Secondary Schooling. *British Journal of Special Education*, 42(2): 128–51.

Ofsted (2012a) *No Place for Bullying: How Schools Create a Positive Culture and Prevent and Tackle Bullying.* London: HMSO.

Ofsted (2012b) *The Pupil Premium: How Schools are Using the Pupil Premium Funding to Raise Achievement for Disadvantaged Pupils.* London: Ofsted.

Ofsted (2013) *Unseen Children: Access and Achievement 20 Years On: Evidence Report.* Manchester: Ofsted. [Online]. Retrieved from: www.gov.uk/government/uploads/system/uploads/attachment_data/file/379157/Unseen_20children_20-_20access_20and_20achievement_2020_20years_20on.pdf (accessed 23 April 2017).

Ofsted (2014) *Pupil Premium: An Update.* London: Ofsted.

Perry, C (2016) *Special Educational Needs: A Brief Overview.* Northern Ireland Assembly. [Online]. Retrieved from: www.niassembly.gov.uk/globalassets/documents/raise/publications/2016-2021/2016/education/5116.pdf (accessed 23 April 2017).

Rayner, G (2017) *Theresa May Unveils Plans for New Generation of Grammar Schools.* [Online]. Retrieved from: www.telegraph.co.uk/news/2017/03/07/theresa-may-unveils-plans-new-generation-grammar-schools (accessed 23 April 2017).

Richards, L, Garratt, E, Heath, AF, Anderson, L and Altintaş, E (2016) *The Childhood Origins of Social Mobility: Socio-Economic Inequalities and Changing Opportunities.* Social Mobility Commission Centre for Social Investigation. Oxford: Nuffield College, Oxford University.

Rivers, I and Noret, I (2010) 'I h8 u': Findings from a Five-Year Study of Text and Email Bullying. *British Educational Research Journal*, 36(4): 643–71.

Scope (2017) *The Social Model of Disability: What is it and Why is it Important?* [Online]. Retrieved from: www.scope.org.uk/about-us/our-brand/social-model-of-disability (accessed 23 April 2017).

SecEd (2014) *The SEN Code of Practice Explained.* [Online]. Retrieved from: www.sec-ed.co.uk/best-practice/the-sen-code-of-practice-explained1 (accessed 23 April 2017).

Smith, PK (2014) *Understanding School Bullying: Its Nature and Prevention Strategies.* London: Sage.

Smith, PK and Brain, P (2000) Bullying in Schools: Lessons from Two Decades of Research. *Aggressive Behaviour*, 26: 1–9.

Social Mobility Commission (2016) *State of the Nation 2016: Social Mobility in Great Britain.* London: HMSO.

Sutton Trust (2015) *Pupil Premium: Next Steps.* [Online]. Retrieved from: http://pupilpremiumsummit.com/report (accessed 23 April 2017).

Sutton Trust (2016) *Social Mobility.* [Online]. Retrieved from www.suttontrust.com/about-us/us/social-mobility (accessed 23 April 2017).

TES (2003) *Warnock Calls for Rethink.* [Online]. Retrieved from: www.tes.com/news/tes-archive/tes-publication/warnock-calls-rethink (accessed 23 April 2017).

Warnock, M (1978) *Special Educational Needs: Report of the Committee of Enquiry into [the] Education of Handicapped Children and Young People.* London: HMSO.

Leadership, management, teamwork and quality

Maintained schools

Academies and free schools

Other types of schools

Educational structures

Inspections

Role of leadership in schools

Accountability and quality assurance

Leadership, management, teamwork and quality

Leadership and management

Effective teamwork

Examples of leadership styles applicable to educational settings

Educational leadership and management

INTRODUCTION

This chapter starts by examining a range of school structures before moving on to consider how these organisations are led. Schools need a robust leadership and management structure and it is vital that the right leadership style is selected to meet each institution's specific needs. Additionally, this chapter considers team-working for the leader and characteristics of effective teams will be examined. Finally, the quality assurance process that underpins effective leadership and management will be studied, with a short critique of current systems.

SUBJECT EXPERTISE LINKS

This chapter helps you work towards the following QAA (2015) *Subject Benchmark Statement: Education Studies* standards:

Knowledge and understanding

○   The underlying values, theories and concepts relevant to education.

○   The diversity of learners and the complexities of the education process.

○   The societal and organisational structures and purposes of educational systems, and the possible implications for learners and the learning process.

Transferable skills

Working with others

○   Collaborate and plan as part of a team, to carry out roles allocated by the team and take the lead where appropriate, and to fulfil agreed responsibilities.

Application

○   Use a range of evidence to formulate appropriate and justified ways forward and potential changes in practice.

OBJECTIVES

This chapter develops your understanding of:

○   school systems;

○   the school quality assurance system;

○   educational theories of leadership;

○   characteristics of teamwork.

EDUCATIONAL STRUCTURES

England has a complex arrangement of school types operating within its education system. Cambridge County Council (2016) provide a useful explanation of these, which has been outlined as follows.

Maintained schools

The majority of schools are still maintained schools, although academies will continue to grow. There are four main types of maintained schools: community schools, foundation and trust schools, voluntary aided (VA) schools and voluntary controlled schools. The majority of primary schools are still maintained but they are in a minority now at secondary level as academies continue to grow as a result of governmental policy. Maintained schools have support services available from the local authority (LA) such as in relation to behaviour support. The differences are outlined in Table 6.1.

Table 6.1 Maintained schools

Maintained school type	What they are	How they are run	How they are funded	Curriculum
Community schools	Schools controlled by the LA	LA has overall control over staffing and admissions.	LA budget	National curriculum (NC)
Foundation and trust schools	Schools controlled by the governing body	Governing body has control over staffing and admissions.	LA budget	NC
Voluntary aided schools	Mainly faith schools	Governing body has control over staffing and admissions. Religion may impact on admissions and staffing policy.	Mainly LA; small amount from a foundation or trust (linked to the faith aspect)	NC and religious focus on the faith associated with the school
Voluntary controlled schools	Like VA schools but run by LA	LA has control over staffing and admissions. Religion may impact on admissions and staffing policy.	LA	NC and may have religious focus

Academies and free schools

Academies are also publicly funded schools and have either converted from maintained schools or been set up by sponsors in partnership with the Department for Education (DfE) and are run by a governing body or academy trust. They are held accountable through a funding agreement and in some cases the starting point is a failing school. They are not answerable to the LA and have freedom to determine aspects such as school hours, term dates and pay and conditions of the staff, and they do not have to follow the national curriculum. Academies must buy in outside help when needed such as in relation to special educational needs and disability (SEND), although they do receive funding for this. They must follow the same rules as LA schools in relation to admissions and exclusions, and where joined in a group they are known as Multi-Academy Trusts (MATs). The aim of academies is to raise standards in the school and increase achievement. However, the irony of the situation should be considered and is well described by Hattie (2015) who suggests that:

> *a popular solution to claims about 'failing schools' is to invent new forms of schools. There is a remarkable hunger to create... free schools, academies, public–private schools – anything other than a public school. But, given that the variance in stu-dent achievement between schools is small relative to variance within schools, it is folly to believe that a solution lies in different forms of schools... This lack of a marked effect is surely not surprising when it is realised that within a year or so the 'different' school becomes just another school, with all the usual issues that confront all schools.*

(Hattie, 2015, p 23)

Free schools are state-funded, not-for-profit schools established in response to local demands by organisations such as universities, charities and parents with the intention of enabling a better choice of provision in their local area. They do not need an existing school building and have similar levels of autonomy as academies. They must, however, adhere to the legal requirements around such things as SEND provision. Although the government claims they increase choice to help improve standards, critics suggest they will be disproportionately represented in middle-class areas, attracting the best pupils at the expense of other schools in the area (BBC, 2015).

Other types of schools

Table 6.2 Other types of schools

Other types of schools	What they are	How they are run	How they are funded	How they are set up	How children are selected	Curriculum
Public grammar schools (also maintained schools)	State-funded schools	LA controlled	Publicly funded	Set up under 1944 Education Act when a three-tier system of secondary education came about	Academic ability	NC
Independent schools	Schools that charge a fee	By the governing body	Fees, donations	Many were set up by foundations many years ago or founded by new charities or companies	Often academic ability but can be financial	Do not need to follow NC

State grammar schools, where entry is based on academic selection, exist in some LAs but the current government's Green Paper *Schools that Work for Everyone* (DfE, 2016) outlines plans to reintroduce them nationally. This move is strongly opposed by many educationalists including the previous education secretary Nicky Morgan, who claim that they may decrease social mobility (Morgan et al., 2017). There are also a number of independent (fee-paying) schools that exist around England, which must be registered with the DfE. More detail can be seen in Table 6.2.

LEADERSHIP AND MANAGEMENT

Activity

What do you think is the difference between leadership and management?

Schedlitzki and Edwards (2014, p 14) debate these terms in detail but quote a number of sources to distinguish between them as follows:

We manage things, but we lead people

(attributed to John Adair)

The manager administers, the leader innovates; the manager is a copy, the leader is an original; the manager maintains, the leader develops.

(Bennis, 1989, p 45)

This suggests that leaders are something more than managers although Glatter (2014) argues that it is difficult to view the terms separately, being unhelpful to divide them into distinct categories. While *leadership* may suggest vision and *management* suggests implementation, both are needed for the successful running of any organisation, including schools. The distinction that is often made between tasks such as improving student outcomes (leadership) and finance (management) should be viewed as interrelated as the management aspects are important for the whole process, which is often seen as involving leadership (Bush and Glover, 2003).

Recently, leadership rather than management has been promoted as being a key feature of a successful organisation. The 1980s saw rapid growth in the area of educational management and the government introduced management training for heads (Bush, 2011). Further development came in the 1990s with the rise of the professional role of head teachers and leadership and management training was introduced in the form of the National Professional Qualification for Headship (NPQH). From 2009 this qualification became a prerequisite requirement for headship and was usually undertaken in the 18 months or so before a person felt ready for headship (Bush, 2011). However, in 2012 the requirement to have NPQH was removed and it is now viewed as an optional qualification again (National College for Teaching and Leadership, 2016). For full details see www.gov.uk/guidance/national-professional-qualification-for-senior-leadership-npqsl.

Activity

What characteristics would you expect in a good leader?

According to Kouzes and Posner (cited in Griffith and Dunham, 2015), there are five key characteristics of good leaders:

1   **Model the way**, which includes traits of honesty and integrity.

2   **Inspire a shared vision** that is detailed and comprehensive and encourage others to take it on board.

3   **Challenge the process** and ascertain what, if anything, is not working.

4   **Enable others to act** by fostering collaboration and trust.

5   **Encourage the heart** by acknowledging individual contribution as well as group effort.

Role of leadership in schools

So what is the overall aim or purposes of leaders in school? There is a relationship between leadership and how it influences teaching and the overall culture of the school (Day et al., 2009). The DfE (2015) suggests leadership ensures the best outcomes for all students, although Fullan (2001) would argue this is indirectly achieved by motivating staff, which therefore improves the quality of teaching and learning in classrooms. It is, however, considered to be so important that there is a great deal of focus on leadership and management in school inspection systems.

Educational leadership and management

There are numerous theories in relation to leadership that have developed over the years and you can use a reputable site to research these on the internet for some of the well-known models such as McGregor's Theory X and Theory Y; Adair; the Hersey-Blanchard Model of Leadership and Lewin, Lippett and White's autocratic, democratic and laissez-faire models. However make sure you utilise academic sources if needed. Many of these earlier leadership and management models are American, having foundations in military organisations, which have been applied to schools and colleges with varying results.

Schools and colleges are complex organisations and it should come as no surprise to realise that one person cannot do this on their own. Educational management is therefore about managing educational organisations and therefore forming an agreed definition is difficult. Bush (2011, p 1) quotes Bolam (1999) who describes educational management as *an executive function for carrying out agreed policy*, whereas educational leadership is *the responsibility for policy formulation and, where appropriate, organisational transformation*. While Bush (2011, p 1) himself suggests that *educational management should be concerned with the purpose or aims of education*. So it is also important that management tasks are linked to the overall aims of the setting to help guide the establishment forward. It is also vital to ensure the right focus for the school; what is needed rather than the plethora of external, government-driven initiatives (Bush, 2011). Bush

(2011), however, does not make a clear definition of educational leadership; rather, he discusses leadership in terms of its influence, values and vision. He suggests that any member could influence others in a school setting without being in a position of authority. Citing Day, Harris and Hadfield (2001), he suggests that leaders convey a sound set of values that are linked to the requirements of the school. Finally, he comments that many leaders are expected to have a clear vision and sense of purpose for their schools but reflects that a unique stance here is unlikely as heads will closely align with governmental aims that are also what the Office for Standards in Education, Children's Services and Skills (Ofsted) will be looking for. Leadership is, however, extremely important in education and Leithwood et al. (2006) indicate it is the second greatest impact, after classroom teaching, on student learning.

Examples of leadership styles applicable to educational settings

As already mentioned, there are numerous leadership models but some are much more relevant in education than others even though it is possible to identify aspects of some of the more well-known ones, such as that proposed by Lewin, Lippett and White, on an individual basis. Bush and Glover (2014) review nine models that relate to education and three of these: transformational leadership, distributed leadership and participative leadership, will be described in more detail below. It has been widely accepted that complicated organisations cannot be led by one person alone and models of shared leadership are those more usually associated with schools.

Transformational leadership

Transformational leadership has been examined in relation to other organisational contexts and key contributor Bass (1990) saw transformational leadership in terms of its impact on followers. A transformational leader inspires a team to put the needs of the organisation beyond their own and to fully accept the aims of the organisation. He suggested that transformational leadership is based on four components:

1 charismatic or idealised influence;

2 inspirational motivation;

3 intellectual stimulation;

4 individualised consideration.

In an educational context, school leaders aim to influence the educational establishment's outcomes rather than actually directing those outcomes. When the model works in an effective way, it enables a united approach to school development. Leithwood (1994) suggests transformational leadership is demonstrated in a number of ways:

o   builds school vision;

o   establishes goals;

o   provides intellectual stimulation;

o   offers personalised support;

○　models best practice and the organisation's values;

○　demonstrates expectations of high performance;

○　creates a productive culture;

○　develops structures that allow inclusion in decision-making.

Transformational leadership aims to alter employees' values, motivating them to perform above expectations. Leaders should aim to ensure staff are stimulated and share the school vision (Vermeulen et al., 2015). They must place the school's interests above their own, and this style relies on inspirational leaders who lead by example (Griffith and Dunham, 2015). The key is how leaders influence the school's outcomes rather than the minutiae of how they actually get there (Bush, 2011). It is about developing dedication and trust among team members (Leithwood and Jantzi, 2005); there is a need to engage staff and other stakeholders in increased levels of commitment to achieve goals (Bush, 2011). It relies on structure, rewards and accountability to enable tasks to be completed (Griffith and Dunham, 2015). This style aims for group members to volunteer rather than be coerced and work with individuals' skills and expertise in order to empower members and increase commitment. It is not just delegation by another name or a way of making staff do more work (Harris, 2013).

However, one criticism of the English educational system is that government policies are often uncritically promoted and adhered to by school leaders, preventing schools being truly transformational in a centralised, government-controlled education system. Governments that are, incidentally, quick to dismiss the views of research specialists (Alexander, 2016). Bush (2011) suggests that if leaders impose their own values too strongly, or those of the government, then this cannot be truly transformational leadership even though on the surface it may appear so. This theory promotes the importance of values but these values need to be shared and agreed by the staff, for the benefit of the school, and not just be the values of the school leader or the government, which is often the case (Bush and Glover, 2014). Transformational leadership works well when there is less external prescription and with the increase of academy schools, and the autonomy that comes with them, this model could be increasingly possible. However, Ofsted will still scrutinise academy schools and is likely to be closely aligned to the current governmental thinking.

Distributed leadership

This style is very much a shared approach to leadership and is in sharp contrast to the idea of one person in charge of the organisation or chain of organisations and recognises there are multiple sources of influence within it (Harris, 2013). This is currently a popular style in educational establishments (Bush and Glover, 2014). Distributed leadership involves working with staff's expertise within the school and can be viewed as a division of labour. Citing work by Harris and Chapman (2002), Bush (2011) demonstrates how distribution of power is not just delegation, noting that the school leaders need to develop the process by enabling space for it to happen. Day et al. (2009) suggest distributed leadership is extremely important for improved pupil achievement and school success. However, formal structures in schools can act as a barrier to distributed leadership, restricting its introduction and implementation (Bush and Glover, 2014).

For distributed leadership to work in practice Kangas, Venninen and Ojala (2016) recommend that staff need meeting time for implementation. However, this is difficult given teacher workloads. Additionally they suggest the organisation must also allow individuals to take the initiative. However, considering that ultimate responsibility sits with the school leader, there are certain aspects of their role that they are reluctant to delegate (Bush, 2011). This indicates there is still a hierarchy in distributed leadership; Harris (2013) notes there can be issues around power, authority and inequality. Research by Leithwood et al. (2006) suggested successful school leadership *has a greater influence on schools and students when it is widely distributed*; however, *Some patterns of distribution are more effective than others* (Leithwood et al., 2006, p 3). The main barrier to distributed leadership comes in the form of the existing structures in schools, which are hierarchical in nature (Bush, 2011).

Participative leadership

Participative leadership, also known as democratic leadership, is about staff having the opportunity to get involved with the decision-making of the school. This was a popular approach in the later part of the twentieth century (Bush and Glover, 2014). According to Leithwood, Jantzi and Steinbach (1999), participative leadership is based on three main criteria.

1. School effectiveness will be increased by greater staff participation.

2. Increasing staff participation is based on the concept of democracy.

3. There is the potential for leadership to be available for any eligible member of the school.

This style allows staff to work together more cohesively while reducing the workload for school leaders and is an effective way to develop team-working. It is thought that staff will be more likely to agree with and apply the decisions they have been involved with, more especially if these have a direct impact on their own role (Savery et al., cited in Bush, 2011). Bush (2011) also suggests that other stakeholders can get involved in the decision-making for the school but the drawbacks relate to the time needed in order for collaboration to take place. In addition, the overall school leader remains accountable for the decisions made in this way (Bush, 2011).

Ultimately the leadership style needed for a school has to link with organisational goals, which should be expected to include pupil outcomes. Good leadership is about the impact on staff (Leithwood and Jantzi, 2006) and focus (Vermeulen et al., 2015).

EFFECTIVE TEAMWORK

As can be seen from many of the discussions around leadership, the team that is led needs to be well motivated and on board with any initiatives in order to drive success.

Activity

What is a team?

Teams exist to accomplish specific tasks that are related to a common goal. In order for people to do this they must interact with one another in some form or fashion in order to accomplish those tasks.

(Griffith and Dunham, 2015, p 3)

For a team to be successful they need to have a sense of belonging and understanding of how they contribute to meeting desired outcomes (Stacey, 2009). Griffith and Dunham (2015) also explore the characteristics of trust, identity and collective efficacy that are considered to be a requirement. Ultimately, an organisation will have a set of values that underpins its vision (Stacey, 2009) so clear understanding of this is vital for a successful team. Teams also need to ensure they have a mix of people with different characteristics to maximise their efficiency. Additionally, Belbin, a leading researcher in this field, considers teams need a range of people with different characteristics (Belbin Associates, 2015). He identifies key roles that will not be discussed here but of importance to note is that leaders and team members need to understand each other's strengths and weaknesses and value what they bring to the team. Team leaders have the important task of making sure teams work in a positive way and complement each other.

Adair is another well-known theorist who wrote on leadership and teams. In relation to teams he considered that there were three key areas that need to work in harmony: developing the needs of the individual, the team and the job or task in hand. This is often represented as interlocking circles, suggesting they should be in equal proportion for a well-functioning team, with a leader's role being to ensure this (Adair, 1987). As far as a team is concerned in a school setting, it is important that there is a good mix of specialisms and knowledge, with people who are dependable as well as individuals who are creative and willing to try new things. Individuals need developing in relation to their particular role in the school and the whole school team may need shared development for a collective approach to be taken towards a shared goal. This collective goal in education often relates to outcomes for students but there will be smaller tasks along the way that smaller teams will get involved in and work together to achieve. It is important that good working relationships exist, as this makes task completion easier as people are more willing.

ACCOUNTABILITY AND QUALITY ASSURANCE

There are many ways schools are held accountable; the government requires maintained schools to publish information such as admissions arrangements, policies and details about their curriculum. Additionally they must provide a link to national performance tables. Academies and free schools also need to publish their funding agreement (DfE, 2016). Schools also need to undertake self-evaluations to demonstrate an understanding of such things as their strengths and weaknesses and data such as that helps schools analyse their performance data. In addition, all schools are inspected.

Inspections

Ofsted is responsible for carrying out inspections of all regulated services that are involved in the care of children in England. Ofsted is an impartial body that reports directly to Parliament, having been formed following the Education (Schools) Act 1992. Ofsted has undergone various developments since its inception and its remit has extended to include Early Years, children's services and colleges. Schools and nurseries are usually informed the afternoon before an inspection but colleges usually get two days' notice, although all establishments can have inspections with no warning. The categories children's provision can be awarded are outstanding (1), good (2), requires improvement (3) and inadequate (4). The frequency of subsequent inspections is related to the grade received. Ofsted makes judgements based on the following criteria:

○ effectiveness of leadership and management;

○ quality of teaching, learning and assessment;

○ personal development, behaviour and welfare;

○ outcomes for children and learners;

○ the effectiveness of early years and sixth form provision where applicable.

These are used to make an overall judgement (Ofsted, 2016). Full details are available in the *School Inspection Framework* (Ofsted, 2016), which is updated regularly so it is important to have the latest version. Much of the inspector's time is taken up examining the systems and procedures in the school, so the self-assessment documentation, which identifies strengths and areas for development, alongside the school improvement plan, are key. After inspection, a report is written and made publicly available on Ofsted's website.

Who inspects an independent school depends on which organisation they are affiliated to. Schools affiliated to the Independent Schools Council (ISC) will be inspected by the Independent School Inspectorate (ISI) but independent schools can also be inspected by the Schools Inspectorate Service (SIS) as well as Ofsted. Both specific independent school inspectorates are approved by the DfE and monitored by Ofsted. Both have handbooks and have a set of standards from which to make their judgements (ISI, 2017; SIS, 2017). These can be seen in Table 6.3.

Table 6.3

ISI	SIS
• achievement	• the quality of education
• the curriculum	• pupils' personal development
• teaching	• safeguarding
• pupils' personal development and pastoral care	• leadership, management and governance
• welfare, health and safety	• the effectiveness of Early Years (if applicable)
• governance, leadership and management	
• early years (if applicable)	

The ISI does not make an overall judgement but each aspect is awarded a judgement of excellent, good, sound and unsatisfactory (ISI, 2017). The SIS uses the same gradings as Ofsted. ISI also monitors the welfare aspect of boarding arrangements at boarding schools and is approved to inspect the majority of British schools overseas (ISI, 2017). The SIS also tends to inspect private FE colleges such as those with a Steiner link (schools following a particular ethos based on creativity; see www.steinerwaldorf.org for more information) (SIS, 2017). Both agencies give at least two days' notice of the forthcoming inspection and both will publish their findings (ISI, 2017; SIS, 2017).

Scotland is inspected under different inspection bodies from England. Preschool provision can be inspected by the Care Inspectorate, while preschool, primary, secondary, further education and community education can be inspected by Her Majesty's Inspectorate of Education. Northern Ireland education establishments are inspected under the Education and Training Inspectorate. Educational establishments in Wales are inspected by Estyn, which is the office of Her Majesty's Inspectorate for Education and Training in Wales and includes primary and secondary.

There is much criticism of the inspection system, in particular Ofsted, which has the biggest inspection remit, and there are concerns it actually stifles creativity and produces 'risk averse' schools. However, inspections can identify good practice, allow for comparisons, and to remove them would result in a disjointed system with even more emphasis placed on examination results (Ehren and McBeath, 2016).

SUMMARY OF KEY POINTS

○ There are a variety of educational establishments and there are different structures in evidence that lead and manage them.

○ No one person can lead a school forward on their own and it has to be combined with teamwork, which drives individuals on to perform in a way that provides the best opportunities for children.

○ Focused leadership and robust quality assurance measures both internally and externally can also make the difference between success and failure.

 Check your understanding

1   What is the difference between leadership and management?

2   What is the key message in the different styles of leadership?

3   What qualities are key for a member of a team?

4   What is the purpose of a school inspection?

TAKING IT FURTHER

Bush, T (2011) *Theories of Educational Leadership and Management.* London: Sage. [Online]. Retrieved from: www.gov.uk/government/uploads/system/uploads/ attachment_data/file/219167/v01-2012ukes.pdf. Further insight into educational leadership. For further education and training providers, see Chapter 7.

Griffith, B and Dunham, E (2015). *Working in Teams: Moving from High Potential to High Performance.* London: Sage. For more information on teams.

Hall, F, Hindmarch, D, Hoy, D and Machin, L (2015) *Supporting Primary Teaching and Learning.* Northwich: Critical Publishing. For specific discussion on classroom teamwork.

National College for Training and Leadership (2016) [Online]. Retrieved from: www.gov. uk/government/organisations/national-college-for-teaching-and-leadership. This provides information on a range of resources to do with school leadership.

REFERENCES

Adair J (1987) *Effective Teambuilding.* London: Pan.

Alexander, R (2016) *What Works and What Matters.* [Online]. Retrieved from: www. robinalexander.org.uk/presentations (accessed 23 April 2017).

Bass, B (1990) *From Transactional to Transformational: Learning to Share the Vision.* [Online]. Retrieved from: www.discoverthought.com (accessed 23 April 2017).

BBC (2015) *What is the Rationale Behind Free Schools?* [Online]. Retrieved from: www.bbc. co.uk (accessed 23 April 2017).

Belbin Associates (2015) *Belbin Team Roles.* [Online]. Retrieved from: www.belbin.com (accessed 23 April 2017).

Bush, T (2011) *Theories of Educational Leadership and Management.* London: Sage.

Bush, T and Glover, D (2003) *School Leadership: Concepts and Evidence.* London: National College for School Leadership.

Bush, T and Glover, D (2014) School Leadership Models: What Do We Know? *School Leadership & Management,* 34(5): 553–71.

Cambridge County Council (2016) *Education System.* [Online]. Retrieved from: www4. cambridgeshire.gov.uk (accessed 23 April 2017).

Day, C, Sammons, P, Hopkins, D, Harris, A, Leithwood, K, Qing, G, Brown, E, Ahtaridou, E and Kington, A (2009) *The Impact of School Leadership on Pupil Outcomes: Final Report.* Nottingham: DCSF. [Online]. Retrieved from: http://dera.ioe.ac.uk/11329/1/DCSF-RR108.pdf (accessed 23 April 2017).

DfE (2015) *National Standards of Excellence for Headteachers.* London: DfE.

DfE (2016) *Schools that Work for Everyone.* London: DfE.

Ehren, M and McBeath, J (2016) *Should We Scrap Ofsted? The Pros, Cons and Alternatives.* [Online]. Retrieved from: www.guardian.com/teacher-network/2016/mar/06/scrap-ofsted-pros-cons-alternatives (accessed 23 April 2017).

Fullan, M (2001) *Leading in a Culture of Change.* San Francisco: Jossey Bass.

Glatter, R (2014) *Leadership and Management: Spotting the Difference: Expert Perspective.* London: National College for Teaching and Leadership.

Griffith, B and Dunham, E (2015) *Working in Teams: Moving from High Potential to High Performance.* London: Sage.

Harris, A (2013) Distributed Leadership: Friend or Foe? *Educational Management, Administration and Leadership*, 41(5): 545–54.

Hattie, J (2015) *What Doesn't Work in Education: The Politics of Distraction.* London: Pearson.

ISI (2017) [Online]. Retrieved from: www.isi.net (accessed 23 April 2017).

Kangas, J, Venninen, T and Ojala, M (2016) Distributed Leadership as Administrative Practice in Finnish Early Childhood, Education and Care. *Educational Management, Administration and Leadership*, 44(4): 555–80.

Leithwood, K (1994) Leadership for School Restructuring. *Educational Administration Quarterly,* 30(4): 498–518.

Leithwood, K and Jantzi, D (2005) A Review of Transformational School Leadership Research 1996–2007. *Leadership and Policy in Schools*, 4.

Leithwood, K and Jantzi, D (2006) Transformational School Leadership for Large-Scale Reform: Effects on Students, Teachers and their Classroom Practices. *School Effectiveness and School Improvement*, 17(2): 201–27.

Leithwood, K, Jantzi, D and Steinbach, R. (1999) *Changing Leadership for Changing Times*. Buckingham: Open University Press.

Leithwood, K, Day, C, Sammons, P, Harris, A and Hopkins, D (2006) *Seven Strong Claims about Successful School Leadership.* London: DfES.

Morgan, N, Powell, L and Clegg, N (2017) *On This We Can All Agree: Selection is Bad for Our Schools.* [Online]. Retrieved from: www.guardian.com/commentisfree/2017/mar/19/help-poorer-pupils-selection-social-mobility-education-brexit-grammar-schools. (accessed 23 April 2017).

National College for Teaching and Leadership (2016) *Professional Development for School Leaders.* [Online]. Retrieved from: www.gov.uk/government/collections/professional-development-for-school-leaders (accessed 23 April 2017).

Ofsted (2016) *School Inspection Framework.* [Online]. Retrieved from www.gov.uk/government/publications/school-inspection-handbook-from-september-2015 (accessed 23 April 2017).

Schedlitzki, D and Edwards, G (2014) *Studying Leadership: Traditional Approaches.* London: Sage.

SIS (2017) *The Handbook for Inspecting Independent Schools.* [Online]. Retrieved from: www.schoolinspectionservice.co.uk (accessed 23 April 2017).

Stacey, M (2009) *Teamwork and Collaboration in Early Years Settings*. Exeter: Learning Matters.

Vermeulen, M, Van Acker, F, Kreijns, K and van Buuren, H (2015) Does Transformational Leadership Encourage Teachers' Use of Digital Materials? *Educational Management, Administration and Leadership*, 43(6): 1006–25.

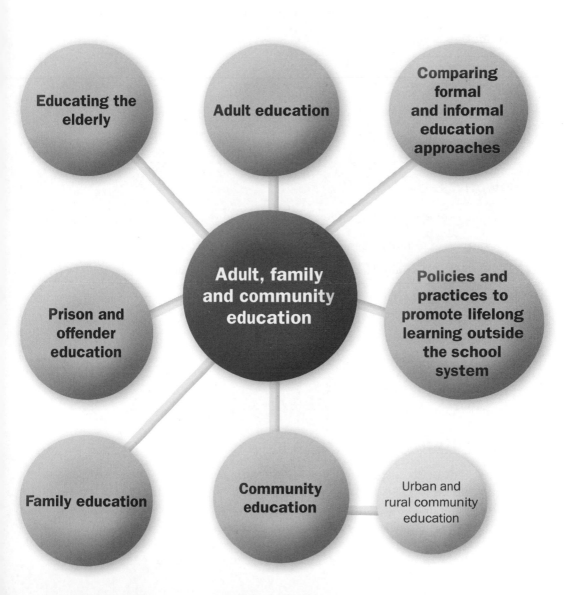

INTRODUCTION

This chapter outlines the diversity of the adult education sector, considering how political intervention has shaped, and continues to shape, this vibrant and complex education sector.

SUBJECT EXPERTISE LINKS

This chapter helps you work towards the following QAA (2015) *Subject Benchmark Statement: Education Studies* standards.

Knowledge and understanding

○ The underlying values, theories and concepts relevant to education.

○ The diversity of learners and the complexities of the education process.

Application

○ Analyse educational concepts, theories and issues of policy in a systematic way.

○ Accommodate new principles and understandings.

OBJECTIVES

This chapter develops your understanding of:

○ comparing formal and informal education approaches;

○ policies and practices to promote lifelong learning outside the school system;

○ community education;

○ family education;

○ prison offender education;

○ educating the elderly.

ADULT EDUCATION

Adult education or, to use another well-known term, post-compulsory education, is for all learners aged 18 or over; although this is sometimes extended to 19 for learners on a full-time education course. After this age, whether a learner funds their own education or not becomes more complex. For example, learners on apprenticeship schemes, learners in receipt of benefits and/or earners who do not have an English or mathematics qualification at Level 2 or above (normally) do not have to pay or pay a reduced fee.

The Adult Education Budget is reviewed each year and combines all Skills Funding Agency participation and support funding that is not European Social Fund, advanced learner loans or apprenticeships.

Activity

Find more information from the gov.uk website about funding adult education.

Funding adult education is, to some extent, offset against savings and benefits in other government-funded areas. The Warwick Institute of Employment Research (2016, p13) cite Fujiwara (2012), whose research found that participation in adult education can:

- *improve health;*
- *provide a greater likelihood of finding a job and/or staying in a job;*
- *help to develop better social relationships;*
- *provide a greater likelihood that people volunteer on a regular basis;*
- *increase employability – more than a third of people ... with no qualifications were long-term sick or disabled.*

Therefore, according to this research, by participating in adult education, some adults may require less support in terms of benefits and access to government-funded services.

Activity

Have you undertaken any adult education courses since leaving school? If so, what and why?

Unless you are under the age of 18, the course you are taking at the moment will be an adult, post-compulsory education course that is most probably delivered in one of the following environments:

- colleges (further education, sixth form or Special Education Needs);
- community learning and development centres;
- universities;
- training organisations;
- industries with their own training establishments;
- prisons;
- public houses, religious centres, museums, libraries and other venues as appropriate.

Within the environments noted above there are around *200 different subjects taught that range from hairdressing to history and plumbing to philosophy* (Crawley, 2016). However, the sector is constantly subject to change and the types of courses offered year on year can vary depending on public demand, geographical area or which education schemes the government is investing in. So complex is the sector that some *commentators have quipped of the resulting landscape of post-compulsory education and training provision: if you are not confused by it, then you have not understood it* (Norris and Adams, 2017, p 3).

The range of courses that are delivered are also, often, delivered at different levels. For example, pre-entry (below a Level 1) to higher education (Level 7). Information about levels of qualifications can be found within the Regulated Credit Framework (2015) – which replaced the Qualifications Credit Framework in 2015 (Machin et al., 2016). Most of these courses will be formal accredited courses.

Activity

What types of courses, and at what levels, are delivered at the institution where you are studying?

COMPARING FORMAL AND INFORMAL EDUCATION APPROACHES

Formal education is a structured education system that delivers a specific curriculum dependent on the age and ability levels of the learners. Formal education is generally provided in schools, colleges, university settings and training organisations. Teachers regularly test learners to see if they are making sufficient progress to attain the required learning outcomes. Programmes of learning are normally accredited by an awarding body (for example, City and Guilds, BTEC, Edexcel) or a university. If learners successfully complete the course that they are enrolled on then they are accredited with a qualification and receive a certificate.

Informal (or less formal) education is unplanned learning or learning that requires no formal testing. Recreational courses, such as cookery, woodwork, crafts, as well as sporting and other activities that develop a skill provide informal education. If literacy or numeracy is embedded within an informal course it might receive some funding from the government; otherwise learners usually need to pay for these courses.

Informal education is also gained through daily activities (for example, personal use of computers, home maintenance, reading and other learning encounters).

Whether formal or informal, all learning supports the growth of a person's social mobility and employability; both of which successive governments have considered so important to the country's well-being that policies have been *recreated on an alarmingly regular basis* (Norris and Adams, 2017, p 3).

Activity

In what ways might social mobility be achieved through learning?

POLICIES AND PRACTICES TO PROMOTE LIFELONG LEARNING OUTSIDE THE SCHOOL SYSTEM

Both the Butler Act (1944) and the McNair Report (1944) included reference to the importance of adult education in developing adults' skills for employability purposes. Around this time mechanical institutes and what later became known as technical colleges offered courses for adults who wanted to gain employment in a vocational or industrial occupation rather than to follow a more academic route (perhaps university). Courses were delivered either full-time, as day release or in the evenings. During the 1970s, technical colleges became known as colleges of technology; this change being due to the growing development and use of technology (Wallace, 2013, p 3). By the 1980s, many of these colleges of technology became known as further education colleges (Wallace, 2013, p 3) and adult education was referred to as the further education sector. In 2007, following a radical overall by the then Labour government, adult education became known as the lifelong learning sector (Machin et al., 2016), although colleges were still referred to as further education colleges.

In 1981, a White Paper called *A New Training Initiative* recommended a *one-year work-related training scheme for all 16-year-old school leavers* (Wallace, 2013, p 19). The paper proposed a shift from traditional time-served apprentice models to an assessment of competence model, which Wallace (2013, p 19) describes as *if you could do it, no matter when you could do it, you got the qualification*. This model was the forerunner to the Youth Training Scheme (YTS); a scheme that became known as training without a job, as it equipped young people with skills without any necessary offer of employment (Wallace, 2013).

Another White Paper (*Working Together: Education and Training*, 1986) recommended that a National Council for Vocational Qualifications (NCVQ) be set up with a remit to develop a framework of National Vocational Qualifications (NVQs). These NVQs were offered to adults within a range of occupational areas and across five ability levels; with, for example, Level 2 being equivalent to a grade A–C GCSE and a Level 3 being equivalent to an A level. NVQs presented opportunities to gain qualified status to millions of adults; some of whom may have chosen an NVQ route as an alternative to a more traditional academic route and some of whom, prior to the introduction of NVQs, had no accredited route that evidenced their levels of competence in their occupational area. However, NVQs have not had

> *any positive outcomes whatsoever in terms of earnings and career progression... the content of many current vocational qualifications is not actually valued by employers.*
>
> (Wolf, 2011, p 71)

By 2010, due to further changes in policy, very few NVQs were being offered.

At the same time as social, political and economic considerations by successive governments were changing the face of what programmes of study could be offered, the way in which adult education was being delivered was also being debated. In 1999, a new national body called the Further Education National Training Organisation (FENTO) emerged that, in 2001, introduced a set of training standards that all teachers working within the post-compulsory sector needed to meet in order to become qualified (Skills Commission, 2009, p 19).

By the late 1990s, when Labour were in power, a frenzy of reports – for example, *Success for All* (2002), *Equipping Our Teachers for the Future* (2004), *Foster Report* (2005), *Raising Skills, Improving Life Chances* (2006) – all stressed the impact that good teaching could have on learners in post-compulsory education. For example, the *Raising Skills, Improving Life Chances* report suggested that:

> *the economic mission of the sector is at the heart of its role… its central purpose being to equip young people and adults with the skills and qualities that they want… including skills and attributes for enterprise and self-employment… and to provide a world class education system that provides a high quality learning experience for all.*

The then Labour government considered that a *world class education system* could be provided through training and the qualified status of teachers within the sector. In 2005 a Sector Skills Council (SSC), namely Lifelong Learning UK (LLUK), replaced FENTO and in 2007 they introduced a new set of teacher training standards with a requirement from LLUK that all teachers employed after 2001 needed to become qualified. This regulatory requirement brought about the implementation of a Diploma in Teaching in the Lifelong Learning Sector (DTLLS) award and a shorter Associate in Teaching in the Lifelong Learning Sector (ATLLS) award; both of which were bound by an associated set of criteria and a set of standards overseen by LLUK.

However, policy changes quickly and in 2012 (during the time of a Conservative/Liberal coalition government) a report by Lingfield suggested that teacher training in the LLS was *distinctly uneven* and that the standards were not *fit for purpose* (Lingfield, 2012, pp 16, 22) and among his recommendations was the deregulation of initial teacher education, which has, according to a report by Belgutay (2017), had a part to play in the 20 per cent drop in the number of enrolments onto post-compulsory teacher training courses. However, removing the requirement to become qualified has not removed any requirement for teachers to meet the quality standards as laid down in the Ofsted framework.

Activity

A report by the Department for Business, Innovation and Skills (DfBIS, 2012) countered some of Lingfield's comments. Locate this report and see what it has to say.

Change, in post-compulsory education, is always on the horizon. For example, since the 1980s there has been:

o   28 major pieces of legislation related to vocational, FE and skills training;

o   six different ministerial departments with overall responsibility for education;

o   48 secretaries of state with relevant responsibilities;

o   no organisation has survived longer than a decade.

(Norris and Adams, 2017, p 5)

With the *Post 16: Skills Plan* (2016) introducing a reformed skills system as well as the introduction of 'T' (technical) qualifications, further change is imminent.

Table 7.1 Chronology of policies and Acts that have impacted on adult education since 2010

Date	Title	Comments
2010	White Paper, *Skills for Sustainable Growth*	This paper sets out the national skills strategy for England.
2011	Wolf Review of vocational education for 14–19-year-olds	This review made recommendations for a change in funding from qualification to student; to improve the quality of apprenticeships; expand the teaching of useful vocational qualifications and the teaching of maths and English; extend the provision of work experience.
2011	DfBIS, Further Education and Skills System Reform Plan: Building a World Class Skills System	This document sets out what is required to reform the FE and skills sector for adults aged 19 and over in England.
2011	Education Act	This Act makes it easier for colleges to make their own decisions.
2011	DfBIS Review Offender Management.	This document makes recommendations for change so that prisoners are developing skills for employability.
2012	*Professionalism in Further Education*: final report of the Independent Review Panel	Lingfield's review of teacher education and subsequent deregulation.
2012	Richard Review	Reviews and outlines the future of apprenticeships.
2014	NIACE, *Community Learning and Families*	This report identifies the impact of community learning on families.
2015	White Paper, 2010 to 2015 government policy: further education and training	This paper sets out reforms for raising the quality and efficiency of FE and skills.
2016	Post 16: Skills Plan	Introduced radical changes to post-16 education including the introduction of technical (T) level qualifications.

Undoubtedly, further change and policy implementation will follow as Brexit unfolds.

COMMUNITY EDUCATION

According to the Skills Funding Agency (2014), community education includes a range of community-based and outreach learning opportunities where people can, for example:

o   get a new skill;

o   reconnect with learning;

o   follow an interest;

o   prepare to progress to formal courses;

o   learn how to support their children better.

Community education is about widening participation by making education accessible to all. As its name suggests, it is most often taught at venues other than colleges or training organisations.

Urban and rural community education

Community education takes place in both urban and rural environments. How a geographical area is classified as urban or rural varies, with some areas being classified on the basis of their degree of sparseness while others are classified on the basis of the driving time or mileage distance to a main town. In urban areas, community education is likely to be delivered in further education colleges or other venues that are situated in a town or sometimes village location where learners can easily access them; for example, public houses, community cafes, purposely rented premises, libraries, museums and religious centres.

In rural locations where the nearest town might be some distance away and any courses offered there not easily accessible due to, for example, childcare, finance and transport, community education is often delivered in village halls, parish religious centres, mobile units, pop-ups and other suitable and available environments in the location.

Community education provides a service for those people who choose or only have the option to access learning through this route.

FAMILY EDUCATION

The National Institute of Adult Continuing Education (NIACE) outlines family learning as *any learning activity that involves both children and adult family members, where learning outcomes are intended for both, and that contributes to a culture of learning in the family* (NIACE, 2013, p 10). As NIACE note, this includes:

o   *parental engagement and involvement in their child/children's learning;*

o   *learning through doing things together (e.g., activities at home, visiting museums);*

o   *inter-generational family learning courses;*

o   *adult-only family learning courses (e.g., keeping up with the children);*

o   *parenthood courses.*

(NIACE, 2014, p 10)

Although the take-up of family learning programmes has been sparse (DfBIS, 2012, p 11), the data gathered from those who have engaged in them provides a positive view of the impact that family learning can have on all members of the family and in particular children's development. Two key findings from a report by NIACE (subsumed, in 2016, by the Learning and Work Institute) were that:

○ *Parental involvement in school is more than four times as important as socio-economic class in influencing academic performance of young people of school age.*

○ *Parents who take part in family learning improve their parenting practices, offer more and better support to their children, take greater interest in and improve their understanding of their children's learning and develop more positive attitudes to learning.*

(NIACE, 2014, p 12)

Like other forms of education, family education is offered in a variety of settings, for example, further education colleges, libraries, museums and religious centres. It is also offered in schools at a time when children and parents can attend.

PRISON AND OFFENDER EDUCATION

It is the prison governor who makes decisions about the curriculum offered in their prison(s). This must, however, include:

○ employability skills;

○ English and mathematics;

○ ICT.

Other courses on offer might include:

○ thinking skills;

○ equality and diversity;

○ addiction rehabilitation;

○ functional skills;

○ a range of GCSEs and A levels;

○ a range of vocational qualifications (hairdressing, IT, painting and decorating, cookery, art).

Tasked with a commission to review the prison education system, Sally Coates (2016, p 4) in her report *Unlocking the Potential*, recommends:

○ *a personalised approach that governors should take in developing education;*

○ *raising aspirations of prisoners by providing opportunities to achieve industry-standard vocational qualifications and access to higher education;*

○ *prisoners' development of ICT and digital technology.*

A rationale gives by Coates for the above strategies is to improve the self-esteem and confidence of prisoners so that society benefits from a decrease in crime and ex-offenders are more likely to seek and to remain in employment. However, some offenders are already well educated and/or have a range of useful skills and have often used these (due to various reasons) for illegal purposes. Therefore, alongside education for employability purposes is a requirement for education for behavioural purposes; for example, courses relating to thinking skills and life skills. Specifically, according to DfBIS (2011) the teaching of life skills is necessary for female offenders as they often have a broader range of complex issues and challenges than do male offenders.

EDUCATING THE ELDERLY

Education is not confined to the young. Discussing the elderly in association with learning could mean adults older than 45 years still in or looking for employment (Tikkanen and Nyhan 2006, p 10). It could mean mature adults, near to or post-retirement age and still working. Or it might mean retired people who want to study for an academic or vocational qualification and/or learn a new non-accredited skill that is taught within a recreational curriculum.

Much of the learning undertaken by older learners who are still in work relates to IT skill-building, which is a skill that many workers, regardless of age, are having to develop and to update. It is also a skill that does not require a person to be at the peak of their physical performance (Laville and Volkoff, 1998).

Why retired people choose to study varies but some reasons might be:

o   change and instability regarding the age in which a state pension can be provided, along with an increase in life expectancy;

o   social and economic well-being associated with learning new knowledge and skills;

o   ability to contribute to society by using new knowledge and skills;

o   health benefits;

o   absence or missed opportunities during their formative or younger years due to child-rearing or the type of compulsory education provision available at the time.

Without any necessity to acquire formal qualifications for employability purposes, many people of retirement age and beyond enrol on recreational courses to pursue a hobby that they perhaps did not previously have the time for. Whereas others may choose to take and acquire formal qualifications, be these academic or vocational. The range of education taken up by older people crosses the full breadth of curricula offered and this includes full- and part-time courses. These courses can be accessed within a diverse range of environments including:

o   University of the Third Age;

o   community venues, such as religious centres, libraries, public houses;

o   further education colleges;

o   universities;

o   social and charitable organisations (e.g., Age UK).

Barriers to studying as a mature and elderly adult can exist. For example, decreases in government funding, courses being too expensive; accessibility issues, travel and transport. According to Age UK, elderly people do not always know what courses are available for them; some have experienced ageism and been told that they were too old to learn and some elderly people from disadvantaged groups think that other people who enrolled onto programmes of learning were already educated (Harrop and Jopling, 2009).

Organisations such as Age UK and the University of the Third Age as well as FE colleges and community education learning centres promote courses that might be suitable for mature and elderly learners.

SUMMARY OF KEY POINTS

o   Adult education is for everyone and a broad range of courses are offered in a variety of settings.

o   The government recognises the influence of adult education on social and economic well-being.

o   Adults can access education on a full or part-time basis.

o   There are more than 200 subjects on offer in adult education.

o   Adult education takes place in a variety of settings in both urban and rural locations.

o   Funding, technological innovations and employer demand for certain skillsets continually influence the offer and take-up of adult education.

 Check your understanding

1   Outline three key features of adult education.

2   Explain why adult education is important.

3   Where is adult education delivered?

4   Who accesses adult education?

5   What types of courses are offered within adult education?

TAKING IT FURTHER

Knowles, MS (1990) *The Adult Learner: A Neglected Species*. Houston: Gulf Publishing.

Norris, E and Adams, R (2017) *All Change: Why Britain Is So Prone to Policy Reinvention, and What Can Be Done About It?* London: Institute for Government.

Scaife, H (2016) A Review of Adult Community Learning in Wales. Welsh Government, nos WG30154.

REFERENCES

Belgutay, J (2017) *FE Teacher Training Falls by a Fifth in One Year*. London: FE Focus.

CeVe (1990) *Pre-Service Training for Community Education Work*. Edinburgh: Scottish Community Education Council.

Coates, S (2016) *Unlocking the Potential: A Review of Education in Prisons*. London: Ministry of Justice.

Community Learning (2017) [Online]. Retrieved from: http://gov.wales/topics/ educationandskills/learningproviders/communitylearning/?lang=en (accessed 23 April 2017).

Crawley, J (2016) *Connecting Professionals: Telling the Story So Far*. Northwich: Critical Publishing.

Davenport, MS (1993) Is There Any Way Out of the Andragogy Mess? in Thorpe, M Edwards, R and Hanson, A (eds) *Culture and Processes of Adult Learning*. London: Routledge.

DfBIS (2011) *Making Prisons Work: Review of Offender Learning*. [Online]. Retrieved from: www.gov.uk/government/uploads/system/uploads/attachment_data/file/230260/11-828-making-prisons-work-skills-for-rehabilitation.pdf (accessed 23 April 2017).

DfBIS (2012) *Evidence of the Benefits of Family Learning*. DfBIS Research Paper No 93.

DfES (2008) *Learning for Life: White Paper on Adult Education*. Dublin: DESL.

Harrop, A and Jopling, K (2009) *One Voice: Shaping Our Ageing Society*. London: Age UK.

Laville, A and Volkoff, S (1998) Elderly Workers, in Stellman, JM (ed) *Encyclopaedia of Occupational Health and Safety*, 4th edition. Geneva: CISILO.

Lingfield, R (2012) *Professionalism in Further Education: Interim Report*. London: DfBIS.

Machin, L, Hindmarch, D, Murray, S and Richardson, T (2016) *A Complete Guide to the Level Five Diploma in Education and Training*. Northwich: Critical Publishing.

NIACE (2013) *Family Learning Works: The Enquiry into Family Learning in England and Wales*. Leicester: NIACE.

NIACE (2014) *Community Learning and Families: CLIF Impact Paper*. Leicester: NIACE.

Norris E and Adams R (2017) *All Change: Why Britain Is So Prone to Policy Reinvention, and What Can Be Done About It?* London: Institute for Government.

Richards, D (2012) *The Richard Review of Apprenticeships*. London: DfE.

Skills Commission (2009) *Policy Connect*. London: Skills Commission.

Skills Funding Agency (2014) *Community Learning, Government Funding*. [Online]. Retrieved from: www.gov.uk/government/collections/community-learning-governmentfunding (accessed 23 April 2017).

Post 16: Skills Plan (2016) [Online]. Retrieved from: www.gov.uk/government/uploads/system/uploads/attachment_data/file/536068/56259_Cm_9280_print.pdf (accessed 23 April 2017).

QAA (2015) *Subject Benchmark Statement: Education Studies*. [Online]. Retrieved from: www.qaa.ac.uk/en/Publications/Documents/SBS-education-studies-15.pdf (accessed 23 April 2017).

Tikkanen, T and Nyhan, B (eds) (2006) *Promoting Lifelong Learning for Older Workers: An International Overview*. Luxembourg: European Communities.

Wallace, S (2016) *A Guide to Policies and Practices*. Northwich: Critical Publishing.

Warwick Institute for Employment Research (2016) *Adult Education: Too Important to be Left to Chance*. Warwick: WIER.

Wolf, A (2011) *Review of Vocational Education: The Wolf Report*. London: DfE.

Type two CE: policy advocacy

Type one CE: large-scale comparative international assessments and surveys

Key approaches to comparative education

Type three CE: peer-reviewed academic study

Comparative education: learning from other countries

Criticise current or past performance to justify education policy reform

Improve education to enhance economic competitiveness in a globalised world

Identify successful approaches that can be adapted

Comparative education: rationale and criticisms

Compare and evaluate performance between different countries

INTRODUCTION

This chapter outlines how national education systems are measured globally, considering benefits of comparative education (CE) as well as criticisms of its methodologies and how findings are interpreted. It then evaluates how CE influences UK education policy.

SUBJECT EXPERTISE LINKS

This chapter helps you work towards the following QAA (2015) *Subject Benchmark Statement: Education Studies* standards.

Knowledge and understanding

o   The complexity of the interaction between learning and local and global contexts, and the extent to which participants (including learners and teachers) can influence the learning process.

Application

o   Analyse educational concepts, theories and issues of policy in a systematic way.

Reflection

o   An understanding of the significance and limitations of theory and research.

OBJECTIVES

This chapter develops your understanding of:

o   key approaches to CE;

o   a rationale for CE;

o   limitations and criticisms of CE;

o   the influence of CE on UK education policies.

KEY APPROACHES TO COMPARATIVE EDUCATION

Comparing education systems is not a new concept. Auld and Morris (2014) point to Marc-Antoine Jullien's eighteenth-century plans for a 'Science of Education' and Alexander (2011), referring to Sadler's work from 1900, argues:

> *Cultural borrowing happens; it has always happened. Few countries remain hermetically sealed in the development of their educational systems, and for centuries there has been a lively international traffic in educational ideas and practices.*
>
> (Alexander, 2011, p 6)

Forrester and Garrett (2016) identify that presently, the growth in the importance of CE studies over the past 20 years is a consequence of nation-states seeking to enhance their competitiveness to meet challenges of economic globalisation. Alexander (2014) identifies three current types of CE studies. Type one, large-scale international assessments, and type two, policy transfer proposals, are closely linked to nations' responses to economic globalisation, with type three representing the continuation of traditional academic studies on aspects of international education. Additionally, there are opportunities for international education exchanges such as those funded by the EU Erasmus scheme (Erasmus+, 2016). These aim to promote cross-cultural understanding and learning from participants' personal experiences.

Type one CE: large-scale comparative international assessments and surveys

Type one research attempts to quantify relative national student ability through achievement tests. The Organisation of Economic Co-operation and Development (OECD, 2016a) organises the following international comparative assessments:

o   Programme for International Student Assessment (PISA).

o   Teaching and Learning International Survey (TALIS).

o   Programme for the International Assessment of Adult Competencies (PIAAC).

Additionally, Boston College USA (2016) organises:

o   Trends in International Maths and Science Study (TIMSS).

o   Progress in International Reading Literacy Study (PIRLS).

Initiated in 2000, PISA assesses 15-year-old students every three years with a rotating subject focus. The most recent, 2015, saw half a million students from 72 countries take part in assessments based on core subjects of science, mathematics, reading as well as financial literacy and collaborative problem-solving (OECD, 2016a). PISA claims these provide transparent, quantitative and comparable data that inform policy-makers of relative education system efficacy: *it's about showing whether school systems are becoming more or less effective in preparing their students for further study or for work* (OECD, 2016b). Auld and Morris argue that such studies increasingly influence politicians of all political persuasions:

> *Riding on the intertwined, and ambiguous, discourses of globalisation and modernisation, and strengthened by their association with economic competitiveness, the surveys have been broadly accepted as 'valid' by policy makers in the 'developed' world. They have simply become too big to ignore.*
>
> (Auld and Morris, 2014, p 129)

While acknowledging that such large-scale studies can provide useful data for further educational research, Auld and Morris' (2014) fundamental concern regards the extent to which such assessments offer meaningful comparisons of education system effectiveness given numerous variants such as size, population, history, economy and culture. Claims of representing relative educational effectiveness are questionable given their narrow scope; not all subjects are considered and evaluation of personal and social aspects of learning is limited. Coffield (2012) further argues that such comparisons assume education systems have similar aims regardless of national and cultural contexts. Alexander therefore strongly criticises the release of international education league tables as a counterproductive distraction from collaborative educational improvement:

> *comparing PISA outcomes has become a political and media obsession, prompting celebration in a handful of capital cities but panic and blame in many more. Meanwhile, PISA's league table format reinforces the belief that... education must be viewed, simply and unambiguously, as a race in which student competes against student, school against school, state against state, nation against nation.*
>
> (Alexander, 2014, p 2)

Perry, reporting for the Northern Ireland Assembly, thus summarises the strengths and limitations of such reports:

> *Both TIMSS and PISA provide a snapshot of pupils' skills at one point in time, and do not provide information about pupil progress. The studies do not provide information about the value schools and school systems add to pupil progress. The results reflect the contribution of a range of factors to pupil performance, including, but not limited to, schools. Other such factors include parental involvement, children's early years, pupil attitudes and socio-economic background. As such, the findings do not solely reflect the effects of the educational system or particular policies or reforms and cannot identify cause-and-effect relationships.*
>
> (Perry, 2017, p 8)

The OECD acknowledges many limitations of performance league tables, recently emphasising the importance of equity within systems as well as overall performance (OECD, 2016c).

Type two CE: policy advocacy

Type two CE reports utilise type one data and other sources to espouse clear education policies, making recommendations based on what they identify as causal factors of success: *It's about taking the results of the assessment, translating them into millions of pieces of data and putting those pieces of together to create a picture of what the most effective education systems look like* (OECD, 2016b). This applied approach to research emanates from international bodies, such as the OECD's interpretation of its own data (OECD, 2016d) and UNICEF for the United Nations (2013), as well as private companies, such as international consultancy McKinsey (Mourshed et al., 2010), international publisher Pearson's *Learning Curve* (2014), education charities such as NFER (2016) and teaching unions (NUT, 2014).

However, Auld and Morris (2014) warn that many such reports come from politically motivated think-tanks and advocacy groups whose work may lack standard academic research procedural verification such as peer-review expert scrutiny, personal interest declarations and transparency of evidence collection and interpretation. Without such safeguards, findings may be more open than traditional academic studies to selective use of evidence and narrow interpretations to push forward their ideological, personal or financial agenda. Alexander (2014) therefore questions the utility of reports where 'success' is attributed to specific factors within an education system, highlighting a tendency to declare unproven causative relationships from data correlations rather than acknowledge a multitude of contributory factors. Indeed, Coffield and Williamson (2011) criticise how education reform has been seen to be a panacea for society's problems, a view exemplified by the then education secretary Michael Gove:

> It is only through reforming education that we can allow every child the chance to take their full and equal share in citizenship, shaping their own destiny, and becoming masters of their own fate.

> (in DfE, 2010, p 6)

However, evidence presented in BBC Analysis (2012) *Do Schools Make a Difference?* and a Sutton Trust analysis of mathematics CE (Smithers, 2013) both argue that education systems play only a limited role in learner success, with influences of broader aspects of society limiting causal links between individual policies and outcomes. Furthermore, policy transfer is problematic when facing cultural/economic differences or faults in other aspects of a system. Nevertheless, such reports may articulate differing, authoritative and often influential proposals for educational development; many authors are highly respected in their academic field. For example, Professor John Hattie's globally recognised meta-research identifies overarching educational traits on behalf of Pearson (Hattie, 2015a). Additionally, the United Nations Children's Fund (UNICEF, 2013) collects and analyses its own research using world-renowned academic experts while simultaneously having an explicit agenda that includes free and fair access to education and gender equality.

Type three CE: peer-reviewed academic study

This relates to research in peer-reviewed academic journals such as *Compare*, *Comparative Education* and the *International Journal of Educational Development*. The focus relates to academics' areas of research interest with policy influence tending to be a by-product, rather than rationale for the study. Auld and Morris (2014) note how this approach has been criticised by politicians for not following what they perceive to be the policy priorities. Consequently, they argue that academic studies receive less funding and attention from policy-makers enticed by attractively produced, if evidentially suspect, policy proposals offering simple solutions to complex problems.

COMPARATIVE EDUCATION: RATIONALE AND CRITICISMS

The following section illustrates key purposes of comparative education engagement as well as outlining critical viewpoints.

Improve education to enhance economic competitiveness in a globalised world

From extensive research dating back to the 1960s, Becker's (1993) human capital theory has strongly evidenced a correlation between educational achievement and economic prosperity. Becker argues that this is a causative link, concluding that education is instrumental in delivering post-industrial economic growth through its ability to deliver scientific innovation, resultant productivity gains and therefore wealth creation. This has influenced policy-makers since the 1980s, where a focus on increasing efficiency to compete in a globalised economy has led politicians to view education as being an essential tool in ensuring national economic survival (Forrester and Garratt, 2016). However, Coffield and Williamson (2011) argue that this consensus has narrowed the purpose of education towards promoting economic gain, with Auld and Morris (2014) adding that the ensuing emphasis of measuring what is quantifiable endangers broader purposes of education, such as equality, social cohesion, citizenship and democracy. Even if the questionable validity of comparative assessments of learners' ability is accepted, to use such results as predictors of national economic well-being assumes that they can also accurately ascertain learners' future economic contributions – even though today's learners may be working into the 2070s. Critics of this direct causative link between education spending and economic gain counter that good education systems may be a contributor to a successful economy or an outcome of one, but are not necessarily the overarching causal factor (Alexander, 2014).

Wilkinson and Pickett (2010) argue that a broad range of social problems for both rich and poor are actually caused by the physical and psychological effects of income inequality. Alexander (2014, p 9) relates this specifically to education, referring to the UK's long-standing record of high income inequality: *Unequal societies have unequal education systems and unequal educational outcomes, thereby entrenching their inequalities.* Coffield and Williamson (2011) concur, arguing that tackling entrenched social hierarchies and unequal access to resources and infrastructure are also vital for universally successful education. If income inequality is a causal factor for education inequality (and this is strongly contested; see BBC, 2010), then education success requires much more than changing education policy but also greater income redistribution as found in successful Nordic countries (Wilkinson and Pickett, 2010).

Compare and evaluate performance between different countries

Despite the disputed validity of international studies, UK government ministers have explicitly linked education league-table performance directly with future economic success:

> what really matters is how we're doing compared with our international competitors. That is what will define our economic growth and our country's future. The truth is, at the moment we are standing still while others race past.
>
> (DfE, 2010, p 3)

Indeed, measuring education efficacy by league-tables was a government manifesto pledge: *We aim to make Britain the best place in the world to study maths, science and engineering, measured by improved performance in the PISA league tables* (Conservative Party, 2015, p 34). This infers a narrow definition of success, as other comparative measures such as the OECD's PIAAC measurement of adult skills are not considered and PISA's literacy rankings are not similarly valued. Even so, this attractive-sounding promise is unlikely to be met in the near future; current UK standing is 23rd in maths, 15th in science (PISA, 2016) and engineering is not even measured by PISA. While league-tables are expedient for politicians and media reporting, even their origin-ator bodies such as the OECD argue against drawing conclusions based on these alone (OECD, 2016c). Nevertheless, fundamental to such large-scale studies is the view that education, as with any public service, can be quantified and meaningfully compared. This strongly links to the New Public Management approach to governance which has pervaded countries such as the UK, United States, New Zealand and Australia. This uses business models to emphasise the importance of accountability and performativity within the public sector (Forrester and Garratt, 2016).

While such apparently hard data may be attractive to policy-makers, attempting to quan-tify a concept as broad as education is problematic and inherently limited in scope; an assessment may give an indication of attainment, but not perceptions, attitudes and ability to later utilise learning. The OECD acknowledge some of these limitations by devising a broad range of assessments, such as the PIAAC (OECD, 2016a) survey of adult skills to consider the extent to which skills are retained following compulsory education. However, the media frenzy surrounding each new data release, fuelled by ideological priorities of politicians and lobbyists/advocacy groups, tends to negate a bal-anced appraisal of international evidence as a whole (Morris, 2015). Given the breadth of education, it is not surprising that UK policy towards children could be deemed suc-cessful or not depending on the choice of measurement focus. For example, Pearson rated the UK 2nd out of 40 countries for educational attainment globally in 2016, but UNESCO 2013 data rated UK child well-being as 16th out of 29 'rich' countries. Even within maths, a subject more amenable to quantitative analysis, Smithers (2013) found a wide disparity in UK performance in the various international studies, depending on what is measured, how the tables are compiled and who participates. Coffield (2012) further questions the ability to make meaningful comparisons between countries such as England and Singapore when the former has around 23,000 schools and the latter just 351. Coffield (2012) argues that within large systems, disparity of provision is more likely to mean that whole-system prescriptions for improvement may not be relevant for all schools. Robinson (BBC, 2014) concludes that such international comparisons are catastrophic for education; rather than informing policy, they are encouraging a narrow form of assessment-led education:

> it's become like the Eurovision song contest of education and we all know what the Eurovision song contest has done for popular music; it's not really led to an overall increase in quality and this isn't helping education either… it's becoming a strategic issue, the stakes are very high and the children whose education it's meant to be are at the very lowest part of the food chain in this process.

Nevertheless, such international comparisons can provide independent benchmarks for education to help evidence whether improved national assessment grades relate to policy success or grade inflation (easier assessments). Additionally, it can provide inde-pendent evidence of characteristics of educational success; for example, finding gender equity in Northern Ireland's maths and science results (Perry, 2017).

Identify successful approaches that can be adapted

The influential McKinsey consultancy reports (Mourshed et al., 2010, p 25) claimed to have found the elixir of successful education: *There is a common pattern in the interventions improving systems use to move from one performance stage to the next, irrespective of geography, time, or culture.* Similarly, the OECD is aware of its impact on global education, arguing that its tests do not just effectively measure educational attainment but can also inform government education policy. By ascertaining key policies within systems it deems successful, it can identify 'what works' in education for other countries to adapt into their own context (OECD, 2016d). Subsequently, the Welsh and Scottish governments have asked PISA to evaluate their systems and make recommendations for improvements to inform policy-making (OECD, 2015, 2017). In Wales, this followed a series of poor performances in international league tables and in Scotland focus related to the renewed Curriculum for Excellence. However, Auld and Morris (2014) warn against blindly following a 'what works' approach of copying successful international systems. They found that where only the best countries are examined, divergence of approaches may be ignored to emphasise common causal features. Furthermore, such a limited scope negates consideration where less successful countries also share identified features without replicating their success – thereby undermining claims to causality. Coffield (2012) concurs, noting that in the McKinsey report (Mourshed et al., 2010), Finland was found to be the top performer but was not included in the analysis; potentially because its education approach differed from the report's recipe for success. Attributing success to specific education systems' features may provide simple solutions to complex problems, but these are not necessarily accurate or able to be effectively transferred where they ignore broader societal issues (Smithers, 2013). Additionally, there is a danger that by seeking to copy those who top the rankings, policy-makers are doomed to playing catch-up with competitors' previous policies rather than seeking solutions that meet the specific needs of their own society. In view of such problems, OECD support for Wales emphasises collaborative working to contextualise reforms.

In England, while league tables have been considered as legitimate measures of success, OECD analysis and guidance has been rejected (Gibb, 2017). Instead, CE has been used to promote selected policy borrowings from different countries such as Sweden (free schools) and America (academies), to justify diversification of schools as part of the underlying philosophy of encouraging a competitive education market. The flagship English Free Schools policy is being expanded while the Swedes are overhauling their system (BBC, 2015), having found this approach contributing to increased social segregation and inequality (Weale, 2015, cited in Forrester and Garratt, 2016). Similarly, the promotion of academically selective schools for 11-year-olds (DfE, 2016) does not follow successful competitors' practice according to the OECD (2016c/d). Indeed, Hattie's international findings (2015a) found policies focusing on diversifying the school system, including free schools and academies, as being ineffective. Alexander (2014) therefore argues that while evidence from CE studies can reinforce political ideology when selectively applied, it does little to change it when contradicting deeply held political views:

Hence the striking phenomenon of politicians praising Finland but then doing the exact opposite of what Finland's evidence dictates: praising a country in which social equity and strong public schooling are paramount and then opting for policies which dismantle public schooling and accentuate rather than reduce inequality.

(Alexander, 2014, p 3)

While citing international surveys to justify change, politicians do not necessarily follow policies in these successful countries, but may use results to push their own ideas about what is required. International surveys such as McKinsey (Mourshed et al., 2010) have argued that 'what works' in education is a high-status and highly qualified teaching profession with a clear training pathway selecting from the best graduates; features shared by successful yet highly divergent systems such as Finland and Singapore. Conversely, England has taken a strongly divergent approach (Morris, 2015), enabling free schools and academies to recruit teachers without teaching qualifications, encouraging assessment only options (DfE, 2016) and removing qualification requirements for FE lecturers (DfBIS, 2012).

Criticise current or past performance to justify education policy reform

In 2010, an English White Paper, *The Importance of Teaching,* started with apparently shocking statistics evidencing UK educational decline: *In the most recent OECD PISA survey in 2006 we fell from 4th in the world in the 2000 survey to 14th in science, 7th to 17th in literacy, and 8th to 24th in mathematics* (DfE, 2010, p 3). Smithers (2013) shows how the previous Labour government claimed policy success based on the initial high rankings, just as the incoming coalition government used the subsequent fall to justify urgent reform. Smithers (2013) notes how both claims were unjustified; the rankings were not comparable due to the initial PISA results being based on a small, unreliable UK sample and with fewer countries entering. Indeed, Morris (2015) argues that league tables provided in international comparisons are over-simplistic and are instead used by politicians to celebrate success, criticise opponents or justify rapid reform without careful evidence building or consultation:

> *In England ... policy-makers have used pupil performance data extensively to justify reform in ways that often seem to be highly selective or a distortion of the evidence. In terms of selectivity, there has been a marked tendency for policy-makers, the media and the network of policy advocates to focus on reports that are negative and serve to portray schooling in England as an educational dystopia in need of urgent and radical reform.*

(Morris, 2015, p 473)

Such (mis)use of international data creating a sense of urgency can justify the need for radical action (Perry et al., 2010), hastiness possibly justified by England having had ten education ministers in the 20 years since 1997; ambitious politicians may feel the need to act quickly rather than thoughtfully.

Activity

Focus on one aspect of education in your country and in another country of your choice.

○ Identify key similarities and differences.

○ Investigate the impact that key differences have on learners and teachers.

○ Consider what issues might be faced if an approach to education were to be adopted by your country.

○ Scan current government education policy documents of your chosen countries for examples where international education systems are mentioned.

○ Evaluate the extent to which any such comparisons are used to inform policy or justify change unrelated to the country/evidence cited.

SUMMARY OF KEY POINTS

○ CE is used to compare relative achievements of differing education systems, although the accuracy of such comparisons is contested.

○ Learning from other countries' approaches to education may be useful for idea sharing and development, although whether individual causal contributors to success can be isolated is disputed.

○ Policy borrowing faces additional difficulties in terms of the extent to which ideas can be effectively adapted in differing cultures/economies/education systems.

○ It is politically expedient to claim to be basing policies on 'what works' from the 'world's best systems', but often evidence cited is selective, being used when it supports underlying ideology or ignored when this is challenged.

○ League tables and other simplified interpretations of complex data may be misused; to criticise opponents and justify hasty reform where negative or to celebrate political acumen where successful.

○ The new emphasis on equity within comparative assessments reveals data about performance within each country based on characteristics such as socio-economic background and gender. This provides independent evidence of the effectiveness of a government's equality and social mobility strategies.

Check your understanding

1   What are the different approaches to international education comparisons?

2   What are potential strengths and limitations of these different approaches?

3   What are the potential benefits of investigating educational practice and outcomes in other countries?

4   What are the challenges and limitations of comparing international educational performance?

 TAKING IT FURTHER

British Association for International and Comparative Education (BAICE)

BBC, *Global Education*, www.bbc.co.uk/news/business-12686570. Regular news updates on education around the world.

BBC, *The Educators*, www.bbc.co.uk/programmes/b04dwbkt. The whole series offers valuable insight, but episodes related to this chapter are: *The World's Best Teachers, What Finland Did Next, Sir Ken Robinson, Professor John Hattie.*

Compare: A Journal of Comparative and International Education

Comparative Education. Academic journal.

Edwards, M (2015) *Global Childhoods*. Northwich: Critical Publishing. Overview of international perspectives on childhood.

Guardian Education, *Global View*, www.theguardian.com/education.

REFERENCES

Alexander, R (2011) Moral Panic, Miracle Cures and Educational Policy: What Can We Really Learn from International Comparison? *Scottish Educational Review*, 44(1): 4–21. [Online]. Retrieved from: www.robinalexander.org.uk/wp-content/uploads/2013/09/ Moral-Panic-Miracle-Cures-and-Educational-Policy.pdf (accessed 23 April 2017).

Alexander, R (2014) *Visions of Education, Roads to Reform: PISA, the Global Race and the Cambridge Primary Review*. Lecture, University of Malmö, Sweden, 4 February 2014. [Online]. Retrieved from: www.robinalexander.org.uk/wp-content/uploads/2014/05/ Alexander-Malmo-140204.pdf (accessed 23 April 2017).

Auld, E and Morris, P (2014) Comparative Education, the 'New Paradigm' and Policy Borrowing: Constructing Knowledge for Educational Reform. *Comparative Education*, 50(2): 129–55.

BBC (2010) *The Spirit Level: The Theory of Everything?* [Online]. Retrieved from: www.bbc.co.uk/programmes/b00v6lkp (accessed 23 April 2017).

BBC (2012) *Do Schools Make a Difference?* [Online]. Retrieved from: www.bbc.co.uk/programmes/b01b9hjs (accessed 23 April 2017).

BBC (2014) *Sir Ken Robinson.* [Online]. Retrieved from: www.bbc.co.uk/programmes/b04d4nvv (accessed 23 April 2017).

BBC (2015) *Education Reforms in Sweden 'Urgent' Says Minister.* [Online]. Retrieved from: www.bbc.co.uk/news/education-33116012 (accessed 23 April 2017).

Becker, G (1993) *Human Capital: A Theoretical and Empirical Analysis with Special Reference to Education*, 3rd edition. Chicago: University of Chicago Press.

Boston College (2016) *TIMSS and PIRLS.* [Online]. Retrieved from: http://timssandpirls.bc.edu (accessed 23 April 2017).

Coffield, F (2012) Why the McKinsey Reports Will Not Improve School Systems. *Journal of Education Policy*, 7(1): 131–49.

Coffield, F and Williamson, B (2011) *From Exam Factories to Communities of Discovery: The Democratic Route.* London: IoE.

Conservative Party (2015) *The Conservative Party Manifesto 2015: Strong Leadership, a Clear Economic Plan, a Brighter, More Secure Future.* [Online]. Retrieved from: www.conservatives.com/manifesto (accessed 23 April 2017).

DfBIS (2012) *Consultation on the Revocation of the Further Education Workforce Regulations – Government Response.* London: DfBIS. [Online]. Retrieved from: www.bis.gov.uk/assets/biscore/further-education-skills/docs/c/12-970-revocation-further-education-workforce-consultation-response.pdf (accessed 23 April 2017).

DfE (2010) *The Importance of Teaching.* London: DfE. [Online]. Retrieved from: www.gov.uk/government/publications/the-importance-of-teaching-the-schools-white-paper-2010 (accessed 23 April 2017).

DfE (2016) *Educational Excellence Everywhere.* London. DfE. [Online]. Retrieved from: www.gov.uk/government/publications/educational-excellence-everywhere (accessed 23 April 2017).

Erasmus+ (2016) *Welcome to the World of Erasmus Exchange.* [Online]. Retrieved from: www.erasmusprogramme.com (accessed 23 April 2017).

Forrester, G and Garrett, D (2016) *Education Policy Unravelled*, 2nd edition. London: Bloomsbury.

Gibb, N (2017) *The Evidence in Favour of Teacher-Led Instruction.* [Online]. Retrieved from: www.gov.uk/government/speeches/nick-gibb-the-evidence-in-favour-of-teacher-led-instruction (accessed 23 April 2017).

Hattie, J (2015a) *What Doesn't Work in Education: The Politics of Distraction.* [Online]. Retrieved from: www.pearson.com/hattie/distractions.html (accessed 23 April 2017).

Hattie, J (2015b) *What Works Best in Education: The Politics of Expertise.* [Online]. Retrieved from: www.pearson.com/hattie/solutions.html (accessed 23 April 2017).

Morris, P (2015) Comparative Education, PISA, Politics and Educational Reform: A Cautionary Note. *Compare: A Journal of Comparative and International Education*, 45(3): 470–4.

Mourshed, M, Chijoke, C and Barber, M (2010) How the World's Most Improved Education Systems Keep Getting Better. [Online]. Retrieved from: http://mckinseyonsociety.com/how-the-worlds-most-improved-school-systems-keep-getting-better (accessed 23 April 2017).

NFER (2016) *International Comparisons.* [Online]. Retrieved from: www.nfer.ac.uk/publications/international-comparisons (accessed 23 April 2017).

NUT (2014) *Lessons from Finland… and How We Might Apply Them in Britain.* London: NUT. [Online]. Retrieved from: www.teachers.org.uk/education-policies/research/lessons-finland (accessed 23 April 2017).

OECD (2015) *Improving Schools in Scotland: An OECD Perspective.* [Online]. Retrieved from: www.oecd.org/edu/school/improving-schools-in-scotland.htm (accessed 23 April 2017).

OECD (2016a) *Education.* [Online]. Retrieved from: www.oecd.org/education (accessed 23 April 2017).

OECD (2016b) *How Does PISA Work?* Paris: OECD. [Online]. Retrieved from: www.oecd.org/pisa/aboutpisa (accessed 23 April 2017).

OECD (2016c) *PISA 2015 Results (Volume 1): Excellence and Equity in Education.* [Online]. Retrieved from: www.keepeek.com/Digital-Asset-Management/oecd/education/pisa-2015-results-volume-i_9789264266490-en#.WGo46PmLTic#page16 (accessed 23 April 2017).

OECD (2016d) *Education at a Glance 2016.* Paris: OECD. [Online]. Retrieved from: www.oecd.org/edu/education-at-a-glance-19991487.htm (accessed 23 April 2017).

OECD (2017) *The Welsh Education Reform Journey.* [Online]. Retrieved from: www.oecd.org/edu/The-Welsh-Education-Reform-Journey.pdf (accessed 23 April 2017).

Perry, A, Amadeo, C, Fletcher, M and Walker, E (2010) *Instinct of Reason: How Education Policy is Made and How We Might Make it Better.* Reading: CfBT. [Online]. Retrieved from: www.educationdevelopmenttrust.com/en-GB/our-research/our-research-library/2010/r-instinct-or-reason-2010 (accessed 23 April 2017).

Perry, C (2017) *TIMMS and PISA.* Northern Ireland Assembly. [Online]. Retrieved from: www.niassembly.gov.uk/globalassets/documents/raise/publications/2016–2021/2017/education/0317.pdf (accessed 23 April 2017).

Robinson, K (2010) *Changing Education Paradigms.* [Online]. Retrieved from: www.ted.com/talks/ken_robinson_changing_education_paradigms (accessed 23 April 2017).

Smithers, A (2013) *Confusion in the Ranks: How Good are England's Schools?* London: Sutton Trust. [Online]. Retrieved from: www.teachers.org.uk/education-policies/research/lessons-finland (accessed 23 April 2017).

UNICEF (2013) *Child Well-Being in Rich Countries: A Comparative Overview.* [Online]. Retrieved from: www.unicef-irc.org/publications/683 (accessed 23 April 2017).

Wilkinson, R and Pickett, K (2010) *The Spirit Level: Why Equality is Better for Everyone.* London: Penguin.

9 Making a difference: practitioner-led research

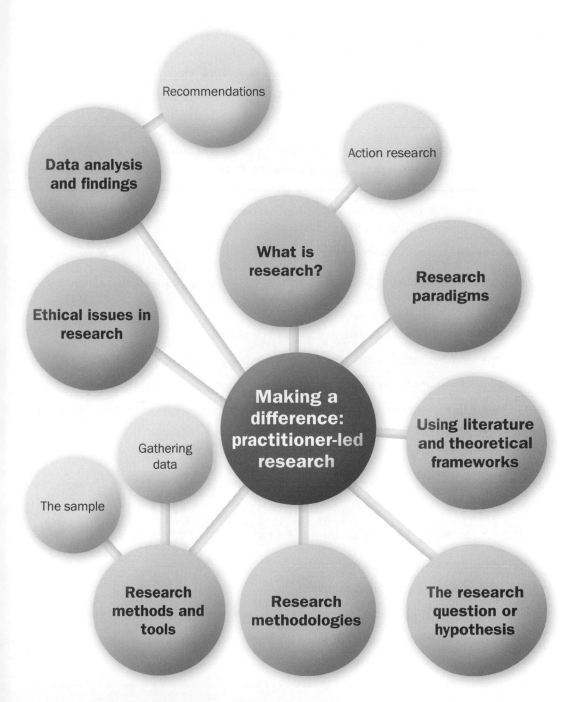

Recommendations

Data analysis and findings

Action research

Ethical issues in research

What is research?

Research paradigms

Gathering data

Making a difference: practitioner-led research

Using literature and theoretical frameworks

The sample

Research methods and tools

Research methodologies

The research question or hypothesis

INTRODUCTION

This chapter explores the role of research within education, focusing on the process of practitioner-led research as a way of improving professional practice. Practitioner-led research also forms a key aspect of many education courses and awards and therefore this chapter explores both practical and theoretical aspects to guide you as a new or developing researcher.

SUBJECT EXPERTISE LINKS

This chapter helps you work towards the following QAA (2015) *Subject Benchmark Statement: Education Studies* standards.

Application

○ Select a range of relevant primary and secondary sources, including theoretical and research-based evidence, to extend their knowledge and understanding.

○ Use a range of evidence to formulate appropriate and justified ways forward and potential changes in practice.

Reflection

○ An understanding of the significance and limitations of theory and research.

Transferable skills

○ Collect and apply numerical data, as appropriate.

○ Present data in a variety of formats including graphical and tabular.

○ Analyse and interpret both qualitative and quantitative data.

○ Articulate their own approaches to learning and organise an effective work pattern including working to deadlines.

OBJECTIVES

This chapter develops your understanding of:

○ definitions of research;

○ the role of research in education;

○ drawing on theoretical frameworks and literature to inform your research;

○ the key characteristics of different research paradigms;

○ different research methodologies;

○   the importance of ethical considerations in research;

○   methods of data collection.

WHAT IS RESEARCH?

You may be looking to undertake research as part of an education-related university course or perhaps just with the aim of developing your practice. Although this might be something completely new to you, it could inform changes to your professional practice, contribute to organisational change or enable evaluation of how far your professional practice varies from your own personal values in education.

First, it is important to clarify what is meant by research and pay attention to specific issues relating to practitioner-led research. Kumar (2014, p 7) notes the *multiple* meanings of research, suggesting that there is little consensus between professionals or academic disciplines. Punch (2014, p 11) considers research to be an *organised, systematic and logical process of inquiry, using empirical information to answer questions (or to test hypotheses)*. Kumar (2014, p 2) takes this one step further, suggesting that *research is not only a set of skills but also a way of thinking*. This next step into practitioner-led research – that is, research undertaken by you as an educational professional – can be particularly empowering (Cohen et al., 2011). There has been a clear move to support and encourage practitioner-led research alongside a national focus on evidence-based reform, noted by Slavin (2008, p 47) *as a drive to ensure that teaching practices are explicitly based on evidence of what works in education*. By engaging in randomised controlled trials – where research is conducted within an organisation, using a control group for comparison – researchers can collect *better evidence about what works best [and] improve outcomes for children and increase professional independence* (Goldacre, 2013, p 7).

Punch (2014) suggests that the increased expectation of practitioner-led research links to the prominence of continual professional development (CPD) for practitioners. He recognises that teachers are not simply drawing on evidence-based research to inform their practice but are *becoming involved in the doing of the research not just the consuming of it* (Punch, 2014, p 45). However, this is a recent development in perceptions of practitioner-led research as Punch (2014, p 45) notes that in previous years, practitioner-led *research was typically seen not to have sufficient academic strength and rigour to convince often sceptical audiences.*

Activity

Who benefits from practitioner-led research?

In considering this question, you need to think about the benefits to practitioner and learners, but also the wider benefits to the organisation, in terms of quality and shared practice with peers. If done well, practitioner-led research can inform institution-wide quality improvement.

Action research

Sometimes practitioner-led research is exploratory or investigative, perhaps a case study that will explore a specific person, or organisation. Alternatively, it can have the aim of exploring the impact of a change to practice. In the case of the latter, research that involves making a change to practice is termed action research. You may choose to undertake action research in which you look to *transform* your professional practice (Kemmis, 2010, p 417). This approach is strongly advocated by McNiff (2016) as empowering to the practitioner and instrumental in driving institutional change. If you are undertaking your research as part of a course of study, you should check whether there are specific requirements for the approach taken.

Action research can be represented simply by a cycle of planning, acting, observing and reflecting.

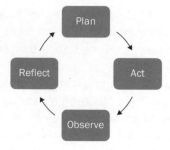

Figure 9.1 The cycle of action research

Activity

Consider an action research project that plans to introduce a new lesson activity to a group of learners. What will occur at each stage of the action research cycle?

The plan stage has already been noted. The act stage is where the lesson activity is introduced. The observe stage is where the researcher gathers the data in relation to the project, whereas the final stage is where you in your dual role as practitioner and researcher consider the impact of the change and explore the next steps, ready to move back through the cycle again if further improvements to practice are required. You may be familiar with this cycle in terms of reflection as an educational practitioner (Kolb, 1984) and Leitch and Day (2000, p 183) recognise that action research and reflective practice, *in their various forms, are considered to be critical dimensions of the professional development of teachers.* However, they note that while reflection is *likely to be related to solving immediate pressing problems of efficient and effective delivery of curricula... practical action research aims to improve practice through the application of practical judgement and the accumulated personal wisdom of the teacher* (Leitch and Day, 2000, p 183).

RESEARCH PARADIGMS

How research is viewed has a key influence on how it is undertaken. This is where the consideration of research paradigms is required, being either viewed within a positivist or an interpretivist paradigm. The positivist, or rationalist, paradigm considers research from an objective viewpoint whereby clear measurements and larger sample sizes provide validity to the researcher (Kumar, 2014, p 14). Machin et al. (2015) concur, noting that positivism focuses on the researcher attempting to take an objective stance in all aspects of their practice. Conversely, the interpretivist or empiricist paradigm has a key focus on *description and narration of feelings, perceptions and narrative rather than measurement* (Kumar, 2014, p 14). The positivist paradigm therefore links to a traditionally scientific view that naturally aligns itself to a quantitative methodology, whereas the interpretivist paradigm links to those in-depth perceptions and views that align to a qualitative methodology.

USING LITERATURE AND THEORETICAL FRAMEWORKS

Any research project must draw on relevant literature and theoretical frameworks. In doing this you will explore any prior research and thus engage more critically with your own project. The literature review plays an essential role in research and identifies not only what has already been written about your area but possible gaps in the research. Although not generally a requirement of undergraduate research, higher levels would expect your project to focus on contributing to the field of study by addressing such gaps in knowledge. The literature review therefore starts before the research questions are formed and continues afterwards. It is a central responsibility for you as a practitioner researcher; its practical applications allow you to clarify the position of your proposed research within the broader body of knowledge rather than being a standalone project.

You will engage with a variety of sources to support your literature review. You might start with books from your library to provide a broad understanding of your focus area, before moving on to peer-reviewed journal articles and conference papers written by experts in your chosen field. These are essential, as evidence presented will have undertaken a robust process of critical evaluation by fellow experts prior to publication. Journal and citation indices are also useful. Journal indices are an online index to a range of journals. They allow you, as the researcher, to navigate through the vast array of journals available and limit the focus of your reading to your chosen subject area. Citation indices enable you as the researcher to identify current literature by inputting an older article to search for. By inputting a source that you have located, a citation index will allow you to see links to more current literature.

A literature review usually encompasses two key elements: a review of empirical research (based on observation and experimentation) and a review of theoretical literature (Punch, 2014). As Kumar notes, the review of literature is not applicable to just one part of the research process, it *makes a valuable contribution to almost every operational step* (2014, p 48). The literature review therefore has a number of roles to play in the research process and these are documented by Kumar (2014, pp 48–9) who suggests that it should:

○   *bring clarity and focus to your research problem;*

○   *improve your research methodology;*

○   *broaden your knowledge base in your research area;*

○   *contextualise your findings, i.e., integrate your findings with the existing body of knowledge.*

When reviewing the literature, it is important to remember that you are not just repeating what it says. As you study at increasingly higher levels, you will be expected to engage with increasing levels of critical analysis. At higher levels of educational research you will not only explore the theoretical literature, but you will evidence a depth of under-standing in relation to the specific theoretical frameworks that underpin your proposed research. This will build on the breadth of reading that you have undertaken as part of your literature review. In doing this, you help to secure the relationship between theory and practice.

The focus on theoretical frameworks requires that you choose judiciously and will pro-vide a greater insight into your research, as Anfara and Merts (2015) note:

> *A useful theory is one that tells an enlightening story about some phenomenon. It is a story that gives you new insights and broadens your understanding of the phenomenon.*

(Anfara and Merts, 2015, p xvii)

There are numerous theoretical frameworks available to you as a researcher, so it is essential that you consider carefully the specific framework that underpins your research. For example, if exploring what drives your learners, you would use motivation theory.

Activity

○   What theoretical frameworks are related to your proposed research?

○   Who are the key theorists?

○   To what extent have those theorists influenced professional practice and more recent research?

THE RESEARCH QUESTION OR HYPOTHESIS

Before commencing research, you will need a clear idea of your aims and objectives. The aim will be broad; for example, to explore the effectiveness of behaviour strategies in the classroom. The objectives will be more focused; for example to identify the impact on learning of specific behaviour strategies, considering teacher and/or learner views. These aims and objectives are the first step in formulating your research question or hypothesis. You will usually formulate what you are seeking to discover as a research question (often with sub-questions) or a hypothesis. Whereas a research question is an issue you are seeking to answer, a hypothesis is a statement, often in relation to a relationship that you are looking to prove or disprove. A hypothesis is usually found in quantitative research, whereas a research question can be used in both qualitative and quantitative research.

> ## *Activity*
>
> Consider the previous example of behaviour strategies. What hypothesis or research question could be used in relation to the research?

A research question might be:

To what extent does a reward system influence learner behaviour?

A hypothesis might be:

A reward system has a positive influence on learner behaviour.

Depending on the size and level of the research that you are undertaking, you might need to break down your research questions further into sub-questions, enabling greater depth. The need to dissect research questions in such a way is noted by Newby (2014) who categorises four types:

Table 9.1 Four types of question (Newby, 2014, pp 272–3)

Who questions:	*To identify a source for the data*
What questions:	*To establish reasons for consequences*
Why questions:	*To explore processes at work*
When questions:	*To establish sequence in a process*

As Newby (2014) notes, not all questions need to be considered for each research project; however, they provide a useful framework for guiding your research question and sub-questions.

RESEARCH METHODOLOGIES

There are three key research methodologies: qualitative, quantitative or mixed methods. At its simplest, quantitative research considers collecting data in the form of numbers, qualitative utilises non-numerical data and mixed methods combines the two.

Quantitative data therefore includes numerical data, perhaps test results, students' ages or attendance statistics. Qualitative data includes views and opinions that cannot be stored numerically. The methodology that you use will align with what you are trying to discover, therefore quantitative and qualitative research have relevance in practitioner-led research, with often a combination of the two (mixed methods research) being utilised. Basit (2010) recognises that mixed methods research can provide benefits to the researcher; for example, the breadth of a quantitative survey can be enhanced by including elements of qualitative investigation to provide greater depth.

Activity

What are the strengths and weakness of a qualitative or quantitative methodology?

You should consider some of the following.

Table 9.2 Strengths and weaknesses of qualitative and quantitative methodologies

	Qualitative methodology	**Quantitative methodology**
Strengths	Provides a deep understanding of the subject area Provides opportunities for the researcher to probe into unclear areas, such as feelings, emotions and perceptions	Opportunities for analysing the data statistically Data can be analysed quickly Easily applied to large-scale research
Weaknesses	Considered by some as less rigorous due to lack of measurability Data analysis can be lengthy and time-consuming Interpersonal skills including interviewing need to be developed Researcher needs good understanding of the potential impact of the researcher on the participants	Strong mathematical knowledge needed to underpin understanding of potentially complex results Often questions left unanswered about the reasons behind the data (no depth)

RESEARCH METHODS AND TOOLS

The methods that you use to gather data filter down through the methodology taken. A qualitative methodology may utilise interviews and focus groups to gather data. However, if you have chosen quantitative research, you may be using a closed-question questionnaire. Indeed, a questionnaire may also have qualitative elements; for example, answers to open questions or different interpretations of scoring scales. You may perhaps use a case study approach in which you solely consider an organisation or an individual's *common or unique features* as noted by Bell (2010, p 19) who suggests that such an approach will help to uncover factors that *may remain hidden in a large-scale survey.*

You may use both primary and secondary sources. Primary data is collected by you as part of your research, whereas secondary data is already available that you choose to use as part of your research. Examples of primary sources may include transcripts of interviews, completed questionnaires or observation documents, whereas examples of secondary data may include attendance records, test results or documents and reports. However, caution should be taken with secondary data to analyse their validity. This is supported by Basit (2010, p 155) who warns that *documents... should not be accepted as unmitigated truth and literal recordings of events that have taken place.*

The sample

You should pay careful consideration to the composition, size of the sample and choice of participants used in research projects. As Punch (2014) notes, a carefully selected sample is essential in both qualitative and quantitative research, ensuring that it is the best suited to answering your research question or hypothesis (Bell, 2010). The sample size should be sufficient to gather the data that you wish to collect and provide greater validity to your findings, but also not too great that it makes the data unmanageable in the timescale available to you. You might use a random sample, perhaps selecting a few learners from each class or year group, if you want to gather views across a school or college. Alternatively, a purposive sample enables focus on a group of learners that you are working with. Whichever you choose, it is important to justify your choice of sample as part of your discussion and whether your aim is for your work to inform just your own practice or to be transferable, informing the whole institution and beyond.

Gathering data

When undertaking qualitative educational research, you might want to gather the views and perceptions of your chosen sample, speaking to a group of learners or staff by creating a discussion or focus group. You might instead speak to participants individually using an interview. Each of these discussion-based research methods may be unstructured, semi-structured or structured. With an unstructured interview or focus group, you may just have a general theme in mind as you start the discussion. You will then be driven by the themes that emerge from the participants, allowing you to explore areas that you had not previously considered. With a structured interview or focus group, you will have clear questions documented prior to the start of the interview, enabling easier comparisons between interviews than if it were unstructured. However, with a semi-structured interview or focus group you will adopt a combination of the two extremes – key questions to consider while also being able to engage with the themes that emerge from the interviewee. Whether you choose to use structured, unstructured or semi-structured discussions, you must decide how you will document the responses; audio or video recording, note-taking yourself or asking someone to take notes on your behalf. You will need to consider the impact on accuracy of information captured as well as ethical and legal issues, especially when recording. For example, consider whether note-taking can capture sufficient and specific data or if recording would make participants reluctant to take a critical stance.

The extent to which you as a researcher have control over the focus of the potential answers from the participants varies along a continuum as noted in Figure 9.2.

Figure 9.2 Continuum of researcher control

Qualitative methods – including interviews, focus groups and observation – are commonly used in educational research. As a research method, observation should be neither intrusive nor invasive: *in naturalistic observation, observers neither manipulate nor stimulate the behaviour of those whom they are observing* (Punch, 2014, p 194). Observation can be considered as a qualitative method, perhaps noting themes that emerge and documenting these as a narrative. However, it also crosses into quantitative research, perhaps with an observer having a checklist or noting a count of observed behaviours. Observation introduces further considerations as to whether the research will be participatory or non-participatory. Most likely, your practitioner-led research will be participatory, recognising your dual role as an education professional as well as researcher, while acknowledging that objectivity may be compromised due to this dual role. However, even in non-participatory observations, the very presence of the observer may cause the class to act differently and may undermine the objectivity of data collection.

Questionnaires can also be used to gather both qualitative and quantitative data and are a popular choice for novice or practitioner researchers both in terms of their ease of use and potential for quickly acquiring data. They may involve open and closed questions, and provide opportunities for participants to rank or rate answers. Likert scales are often used on questionnaires (Basit, 2010) and while the wording may change, they ask the participant to give a view on a scale from 'completely agree' to 'complete disagree'.

Table 9.3 Example of a Likert scale

	Completely agree	Agree	Neither agree or disagree	Disagree	Completely disagree
Do you think that behaviour was managed well in the classroom?	☐	☐	☐	☐	☐

Activity

What scales, other than that of completely disagree to completely agree, might you use on a questionnaire?

You should have considered some of the following.

o   very satisfied to very dissatisfied;

o   extremely important to very unimportant;

o   never to always;

o   excellent to poor;

o   highly effective to ineffective.

Whichever wording you choose, it should have the best fit for the views that you are trying to gather, with the most appropriate language. The questions on the questionnaire should be clearly written to avoid bias or leading the participant in a particular direction. You might also consider whether you will use an odd or even number of options. For example, with three options (such as very satisfied, satisfied and unsatisfied), there is a tendency for participants to opt for the middle option. For this reason, many researchers choose an even number of options when using a Likert scale.

ETHICAL ISSUES IN RESEARCH

Ethical practice is at the forefront of practitioner-led research. As Cohen et al. (2011, p 75) note, this need for ethical practice *is reflected in the growth of relevant literature and in the appearance of regulatory codes of research practice formulated by various agencies and professional bodies.* Two key ethical issues are those of confidentiality and anonymity. Often the two terms are used together; however, there is a clear distinction between the two that you should be aware of. In research where anonymity is assured, the data is collected in such a way that the participants' identities are unknown. Confidentiality, however, is when the participants' identities may be known, but they will not be disclosed by the researcher.

Activity

If a researcher needs to know the identities of the participants, but will not share their identities, is it anonymity or confidentiality that applies?

It is confidentiality that applies. Often in practitioner-led research, the researcher needs to know or cannot avoid knowing the participants' identities. The research is therefore confidential and not anonymous.

As a practitioner researcher, you will require ethical approval before undertaking your project. This may be in the form of a discussion with your tutor or manager or, in some cases, preparation of a case for ethical approval and will need to draw on key responsibilities for participants as noted by the British Educational Research Association (BERA).

1 Voluntary informed consent	5 Incentives
2 Openness and disclosure	6 Detriment arising from participation
3 Right to withdraw	in research
4 Children, vulnerable young people	7 Privacy
and young adults	8 Disclosure

Figure 9.3 Responsibilities to participants (BERA, 2011)

In their ethical guidelines, BERA (2011) emphasise the goal of achieving the *highest ethical standards in whichever context it is needed* (BERA, 2011, p 3). It is these standards that are expected of you as a practitioner researcher.

Whatever your research, there will be ethical considerations. You should think through every aspect of what you are planning to do in terms of the BERA responsibilities, perhaps asking yourself some of the following questions:

○   Have I got written consent from all the participants?

○   Have I clearly and honestly explained the purpose of my research?

○   Have I given participants the opportunity to opt out of the research at any stage?

○   How will ensure that my data is kept securely?

Activity

Think about each of BERA's responsibilities. What other questions might you ask as you consider the ethical issues in relation to your research?

You should have considered some of the following.

Table 9.4 BERA responsibilities and possible questions

Responsibility	Question
Voluntary informed consent	How will you avoid pressuring your participants to engage in your research?
Openness and disclosure	How will you inform participants of the true nature of your research?
Right to withdraw	Have you planned your research in such a way that a participant withdrawing part way through won't have an adverse effect on your data?
Children, vulnerable young people and young adults	Do you need to seek permission from parents or guardians if necessary?
Incentives	Are any incentives that you are offering for participation proportionate? Are you confident that incentives will not bias your research?
Detriment arising from participation in research	How will you ensure that (in the case of two sample research) one group will not be disadvantaged?
Privacy	How will you ensure that the participants and their organisation will not be identified?
Disclosure	Have you considered situations that might require you to override confidentiality (for example in relation to safeguarding issues)?

DATA ANALYSIS AND FINDINGS

You will have gathered a range of data as part of your research. This may be qualitative or quantitative data or perhaps a combination of the two and how you will analyse the data will be dependent on the methods you have used.

If you have interviewed participants as part of qualitative research, the analysis stage is where you transcribe the recordings or pull together your interview notes. You will explore key themes that arise, noting patterns or similar comments to reach a conclusion.

Activity

Consider an interview that explores teachers' views on learner behaviour in the classroom. What themes might emerge from this interview?

While it is difficult to anticipate all themes that might emerge, you might expect discussion to explore themes including those of progress, emotions, responsibility, teacher control and relationships. The actual themes that emerge will in part be dependent on the questions that you ask, with themes developing from a structured interview much easier to predict than those from an unstructured interview.

A recent innovation in presenting qualitative data is the use of word clouds as a visual representation of research themes. This is supported by Edyburn (2010, p 68) who notes that *researchers engaged in text-based data sets [who] may find word cloud tools useful for quick analysis of simple word frequency patterns within one or more texts.*

If you have gathered facts and figures, this stage is when you may choose to use descriptive statistics, for example, mean, mode, median, percentages and range. You will no doubt have gathered a significant amount of data and the descriptive statistics will help you see any patterns and draw sense out of the numbers. You might also consider using standard deviation and more complex statistics including Chi-square or T-Tests if you are confident in doing do.

You might present your quantitative data in the form of charts and diagrams, providing a visual representation of your data. A common mistake that new researchers make is not to consider the purpose of a chart and as a consequence data is incorrectly represented making it meaningless.

Activity

What kinds of charts and diagrams might you use to present your data?

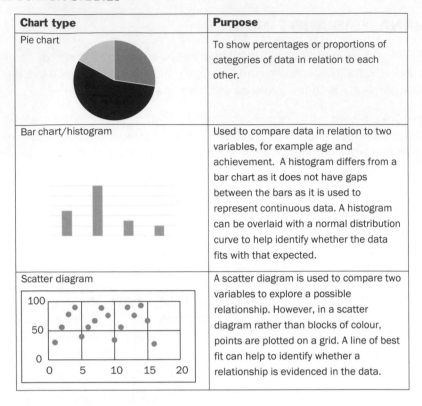

Chart type	Purpose
Pie chart	To show percentages or proportions of categories of data in relation to each other.
Bar chart/histogram	Used to compare data in relation to two variables, for example age and achievement. A histogram differs from a bar chart as it does not have gaps between the bars as it is used to represent continuous data. A histogram can be overlaid with a normal distribution curve to help identify whether the data fits with that expected.
Scatter diagram	A scatter diagram is used to compare two variables to explore a possible relationship. However, in a scatter diagram rather than blocks of colour, points are plotted on a grid. A line of best fit can help to identify whether a relationship is evidenced in the data.

Figure 9.4 Chart types and purpose

You should have considered some of the following.

Recommendations

The final part of your project will look ahead to the next steps following your research. While undertaking your project you will have identified areas for further research or alternatives that you might have explored given the time. As a practitioner researcher, you will also consider implications for your own professional practice in terms of what action you will take as a consequence of your findings or recommendations for your department or organisation as a whole.

Activity

Grace has conducted a practitioner-led research project to introduce an interactive whiteboard activity at the start of lessons with one group of learners. The project was a success and she is looking at future recommendations. What might you suggest?

You might have suggested trying the activity with additional groups of learners, trying different interactive activities or sharing her findings with colleagues and managers. Perhaps future research would explore alternative ways of engaging learners by drawing on what worked well and not so well in her current project.

SUMMARY OF KEY POINTS

- This chapter has critically reviewed practitioner-led research as a key aspect of developing professional practice in education.
- It has provided you with an overview of the various stages of practitioner-led research.
- It has introduced you to the relevance of literature and theoretical frameworks in shaping research.
- It has provided you with an overview of research paradigms and methodologies.
- It has reviewed methods of data analysis and presentation for qualitative and quantitative research.

 # Check your understanding

1 What is practitioner-led research?

2 What are the benefits of practitioner-led research?

3 Why should you draw on theoretical frameworks to support your research?

4 What are the differences between the interpretivist and positivist paradigms?

5 What are the differences between qualitative and quantitative research?

6 Explain why a scatter diagram is not used to represent qualitative data.

7 What are the eight ethical responsibilities of researchers as noted by BERA?

 TAKING IT FURTHER

Wood, P and Smith, J (2016) *Educational Research: Taking the Plunge*. Carmarthen: Independent Thinking Press. This is a comprehensive guide for beginner and experienced researchers.

Baumfield, V, Hall, E and Wall, K (2013) *Action Research in Education: Learning Through Practitioner Enquiry*. London: Sage. An essential guide that explores action research in both compulsory and post-compulsory contexts.

You might also like to explore the BBC's 'More or Less' podcast which looks at data analysis and representation, which will assist in understanding how research is conducted: www.bbc.co.uk/programmes/b006qshd

REFERENCES

Anfara, VA and Mertz, NT (2015) *Theoretical Frameworks in Qualitative Research*, 2nd edition. London: Sage.

Basit, T (2014), *Conducting Research in Educational Contexts*. London: Continuum.

Bell, J (2010) *Doing Your Research Project*. Maidenhead: Open University Press.

BERA (2011) *Ethical Guidelines for Educational Research*. [Online]. Retrieved from www.bera.ac.uk/wp-content/uploads/2014/02/BERA-Ethical-Guidelines-2011.pdf (accessed 23 April 2017).

Cohen, L, Manion, L and Morrison, K (2011) *Research Methods in Education*, 7th edition. Abingdon: Routledge.

Edyburn, DL (2010). Word Clouds: Valuable Tools When You Can't See the Ideas through the Words. *Journal of Special Education Technology*, 25(2): 68–72.

Goldacre, B (2013) *Building Evidence into Education*. London: Bad Science. [Online]. Retrieved from: http://media.education.gov.uk/assets/files/pdf/b/ben%20goldacre%20paper.pdf (accessed 23 April 2017).

Kemmis, S (2010). What is to be Done? The Place of Action Research. *Educational Action Research*, 18(4): 417–27.

Kolb, D (2014), *Experiential Learning: Experience as the Source of Learning and Development*. London: Prentice Hall.

Kumar, R (2014), *Research Methodology: A Step by Step Guide for Beginners*, 4th edition. London: Sage.

Leitch, R and Day, C (2000) Action Research and Reflective Practice: Towards a Holistic View. *Educational Action Research*, 8(1): 179–93.

Machin, L, Hindmarch, D, Murray, S and Richardson, T (2015) *The Complete Guide to the Level 5 Diploma in Education and Training*. Northwich: Critical Publishing.

McNiff, J (2016) *You and Your Action Research Project*. Oxon: Routledge.

Newby, P (2014) *Research Methods for Education*, 2nd edition. Abingdon: Routledge.

Punch, K (2014) *Introduction to Research Methods in Education*. London: Sage.

Slavin, R (2008) Perspectives on Evidence-Based Research in Education. *Educational Researcher*, 31(1): 5–14.

10 Looking to the future: education technology

Curriculum changes

The **historical context of technology in education**

Education technology developments

Looking to the future: education technology

Education technology pedagogy

E-safety and data protection

Education technology, inclusion and social mobility

INTRODUCTION

Computing within education has been part of government policy for more than 30 years, linking learners' ability to use technology to meet changing employer needs and future economic development (STC, 2016a). However, critics such as educational researcher Joe Nutt (2010) argue that the vast resources spent on technology have often been supported by limited and biased research evidence, resulting in limited or unclear outcomes. Nutt and the OECD (2015) highlight the opportunity cost of technology spending, arguing that often this could have been more productively spent on other aspects of education. Other critics agree that education technology has had a limited impact on either policy expectations or meeting employer needs, but argue for greater emphasis on digital skills development to meet the changing demands of the future global economy. Reporting for the Institute for Public Policy Research Scotland, Gunson and Thomas argue that there will be rapid changes to employment requirements due to technological changes:

> *It is likely that increasing levels of automation through technological advances will bring new jobs into Scotland that will require highly skilled, technology-literate workers, while reducing numbers of mid-skilled roles.*
>
> (Gunson and Thomas, 2017, p 13)

Political historian and university vice chancellor Sir Anthony Seldon goes further, considering that the English national curriculum is so outdated that: *We are sleepwalking – Government, schools and universities – into the biggest potential disaster of modern times* (cited in Baker 2016). Institute of Education Professor Luckin, giving evidence for the parliamentary Science and Technology Committee (STC) (2016a, p 13) concurs, predicting mass unemployment if the curriculum is not reformed as the *very things on which we focus our education system are the routine cognitive skills that are the easiest to automate.*

This chapter explores the extent to which past policy has met government, employer and learner expectations as well as the role and extent to which computing, technology and digital literacy may play a part in education curricula of the future.

SUBJECT EXPERTISE LINKS

This chapter helps you work towards the following QAA (2015) *Subject Benchmark Statement: Education Studies* standards.

Application

o   Accommodate new principles and understandings.

o   Use a range of evidence to formulate appropriate and justified ways forward and potential changes in practice.

Technology

o   Use technology effectively to enhance critical and reflective study.

OBJECTIVES

This chapter develops your understanding of:

o the historical context of technology in education;

o pedagogical approaches to developing learner digital literacy;

o problems and limitations of education technology;

o future developments of the role of technology within the curriculum.

Activity

Reflect on your experiences of using technology within your school/college.

o What technology was used?

o How effectively did it enhance learning?

o Did your technology-based learning focus on building and coding computers or learning how to use office-based programs?

THE HISTORICAL CONTEXT OF TECHNOLOGY IN EDUCATION

During the late 1970s, the British Broadcasting Corporation (BBC) ran what they considered to be a successful TV-based basic literacy campaign and therefore sought to repeat this approach for computer training as a response to the first wave of popular personal computers (BBC, 2015). With no preinstalled software, these early PCs required user programming and there was a multitude of brands, each with their own programming language (code), which would have been impossible to teach nationally. Therefore, the BBC, selected one (by Acorn), which became the BBC Micro. Complementing this new popularity for personal computing, government policy led the world in funding computers in schools in the 1980s, with most using the BBC Micro for developing school learners' coding ability (BBC, 2015). With the introduction of the first national curriculum, information communication technology was made compulsory for all maintained school learners aged between five and 16 in the Education Reform Act (ERA) in 1988 (STC, 2016b). However, with the development of commercial software packages, a large part of computing developed into information communication technology (ICT), which tended to focus on how to use pre-existing programs rather than designing and creating new ones (BBC, 2015; DfE, 2012).

In summarising research for international education charity CfBT, Nutt (2010) found that throughout the 1990s and 2000s, many expensive educational technology projects had been launched on the basis of weak, biased and flawed methodology and insufficient evaluation. Nutt (2010) argues that high levels of technology investment have persisted in the face of limited evidence due to a combination of factors. First, overenthusiastic supporters of technology produce reports that fail to meet internationally accepted research standards, overstating benefits or downplaying other potentially causative factors in success. Even where high-quality academically peer-reviewed work is carried out, this may be of limited use due to the rapid pace of change making findings quickly obsolete. Nutt (2010) argues that much of this flawed research has been supported by technology companies out of self-interest, with funding less forthcoming for those with potentially critical investigations. However, educationalist Sir Michael Barber (cited in Hattie, 2015, p vi), while supporting research-informed education policy, agrees that waiting for secure research findings for research-based policy is problematic due to the rapid pace of change: *in a fast-moving world, policy-makers often have to innovate, and by definition, there will not be conclusive evidence either way on an innovation.* Nevertheless, Hattie (2015) finds globally, and Elwick et al. (2013) in the UK, that politicians and education leaders prefer to invest in tangible assets such as new schools and resources that have positive associations with future ideals rather than focusing on more effective training and development of teachers.

Considering the UK as a whole, the Royal Society (2012) and Ofsted (2013, focusing on England) both found that ICT provision tended to focus on specific software training rather than creative application use, design or programming. Both concluded that provision was inconsistent, although primary schools were more successful at embedding technology than secondaries, where many learners found it repetitive and boring. Consequently, rather than increasing to meet growing employer ICT needs, Ofsted (2013) found that English learner numbers had actually been declining since 2007, a phenomena echoed in Northern Ireland (Perry, 2015). Meyers et al. (2013) note how, internationally, digital literacy teaching is moving away from such a technical skills development focus due to the rapidly changing nature of online resources rendering this obsolete. This was recognised by the DfE in 2013, where the new computing curriculum moved away from previous ICT-based basic office skills such as word-processing, to a computer science emphasis on building and programming computers (DfE, 2012, p 1). The Parliamentary STC (2016b) supports the principle of this change, highlighting how it nurtures subject interest, creativity and has potentially broader benefits to science, technology and engineering learning and has encouraged the launch of Code Clubs, which creatively use codeable computers such as the BBC Microbit and Raspberry Pi. Indeed, the move towards coding appears to be throughout the UK, being integral to *Successful Futures*, the Donaldson review of the Welsh curriculum currently being implemented (2015) and also a feature of curriculum and teacher standard updates (Scottish Government, 2016). Perry (2015), evaluating coding in schools on behalf of the Northern Ireland Assembly, also suggests this should be considered for NI.

EDUCATION TECHNOLOGY PEDAGOGY

Meyers et al. (2013) note that the term 'digital literacy' arose in the 1990s from the emergent internet, where the term initially referred to *information* searching and evaluation skills. With ongoing developments digital literacy now needs to encompass online space where users, *create, work, share, socialise, research, play, collaborate, communicate and learn* (Meyers et al., 2013, p 356). Digital literacy therefore encompasses much more than basic reading, writing, speaking and listening skills, breaking out of its original scholarly focus to encompass its key role in culture, society and the economy. Nutt (2010), however, argues that digital literacy does not represent a radical new way of learning and creating but is rather a reinterpretation of traditional higher order cognitive skills of enquiry and synthesis:

> One of the myths propagated by enthusiasts for technology is that the nature of learning has fundamentally changed as a result of wider technological change. They call for a new range of skills, sometimes referred to as 'digital literacy'. The rise of 'digital literacy' as a concept, loose as it is, has also exerted considerable pressure on schools and teachers to change fundamental aspects of their practice and schooling.
>
> (Nutt, 2010, p 3),

Meyers et al. (2013) nevertheless argue that a static definition of digital literacy is impossible as ongoing technological developments necessitate changes to our perception of this concept. They consider that, currently, digital literacy includes practical skills to use technology, cognitive skills development and the ability to use these to meet the changing needs of the individual's personal context. With a multitude of technology easily available, digital literacy is no longer focused on learning to use a single application or piece of hardware but the other way round; being able to select tools to meet ongoing and developing needs, with the OECD (2015) arguing that it can transform learning opportunities through opportunities for interaction and collaboration.

In 2002, Johnson proposed that an online *wisdom of crowds* could further knowledge through a social-constructivist approach to learning; a stance explicitly taken by open-source virtual learning environment Moodle (2017). However, Johnson also recognised the problem of echo chambers, where likeminded people share views only with each other, thereby not encountering verifiable facts to challenge what becomes a repeatedly reinforced prejudiced worldview. In terms of critical thinking within digital literacy, this therefore focuses on the ability to search, sift and evaluate information effectively, focusing on verifying accuracy, currency, relevance and credibility (Meyers et al., 2013). (See Chapter 1 for a detailed overview of critical thinking concepts.) This issue has been recognised nationally by the Growing Up Digital Taskforce on behalf of the Children's Commissioner (GUDT, 2017) and internationally by librarians who are campaigning to educate users on effective searching, with guidance focusing on checking the credibility of the source and author as well as seeking independent verification (IFLA, 2017). Meyers et al. (2013) highlight how the Web 2.0 concept, where the internet is now interactive rather than a one-way information source, has developed this aspect of digital literacy to include creative yet responsible authoring as well. The Cultural Learning Alliance (CLA, 2017) further emphasise the role creative use of technology can have in terms of providing employment opportunities to help counter potential losses from automation. The STC (2016b) also highlight how computer games can be used for problem-solving and decision-making as well as creativity through design and development of self-made games.

EDUCATION TECHNOLOGY, INCLUSION AND SOCIAL MOBILITY

Proponents of education technology have argued that increasing access to information and reducing costs can help to promote social mobility:

> *Basic digital skills are also a powerful social enabler, opening up opportunities for improvements in education, better health care services, connecting people to their communities more effectively and helping adults find work.*
>
> (STCb, 2016, p 8)

However, the OECD (2015) did not find evidence of technology achieving this, conversely evidencing a widening of attainment gaps between learners from different socio-economic backgrounds. The government recognises that digital exclusion is an issue, with its Digital Inclusion Strategy (Government Digital Service, 2014) identifying barriers to access such as a lack of internet access, ICT skills, motivation and trust. Elwick et al. (2013) argue, however, that the digital divide among young people does not relate to a lack of access to the internet, which is almost universal now. Rather, the key issue now is differing abilities to use online resources, especially in relation to completing schoolwork, arguing that the government needs to move away from equipment provision and focus on supporting and training learners to use technology effectively for schoolwork.

In the UK, an estimated 12.6 million people (23 per cent of the population) lack basic digital skills, 4.5 million of whom are employed (STC, 2016b, p 10). The committee also reported that those lacking digital skills are more likely to be from disabled, elderly and low socio-economic status groups, such as poorer families. The STC urged the government to actively tackle gender stereotyping within school computer science, demonstrating how the move away from ICT had actually worsened a gender divide; only 16 per cent of learners being female compared with 42 per cent for ICT, resulting in an ongoing imbalance within higher education. The STC and Baker (2016) therefore conclude that the UK currently faces a digital skills crisis that is damaging productivity and economic competitiveness as ongoing development will replace whole sectors of employment but also create new employment opportunities requiring digital skills.

E-SAFETY AND DATA PROTECTION

All education providers have a legal responsibility for both safeguarding and upholding anti-radicalisation strategy (see Chapter 4). Statutory guidance from the DfE emphasises the importance of monitoring IT usage, stating that schools must:

> *ensure that children are safe from terrorist and extremist material when accessing the internet in schools. Schools should ensure that suitable filtering is in place. More generally, schools have an important role to play in equipping children and young people to stay safe online, both in school and outside.*
>
> (DfE, 2015, p 8)

Furthermore, all education providers will need to ensure their policies and practice adhere to the new General Data Protection Regulation, which is set to replace the Data

Protection Act on 25 May 2018 (ICO, 2017). According to the ICO, a key development of this is an emphasis on increased accountability, where organisations need to evidence how they adhere to the principles of data management. Nevertheless, Ofsted (2015) highlight concerns over safeguarding, citing inconsistent training and out of date or missing policies. Additionally, a report by the Growing Up Digital Taskforce (GUDT, 2017) for Children's Commissioner Anne Longfield (with statutory responsibility to protect English children's rights) argues that school online learning should feature mandatory *digital citizenship*, claiming that present tuition does not sufficiently address the technical skills and legal knowledge required to navigate a digital landscape:

> *Digital citizenship... would include what it means to be a responsible citizen online; how to protect your rights online and how to respect others' rights; how to disengage as well as engage with the digital world – ultimately nothing less than how to make the online world a force for good and one which empowers and inspires children, rather than entrapping them.*
>
> (GUDT, 2017, p 5)

The GUDT argues that the government should also take a stronger lead in protecting children's online human rights:

> *The supposedly 'public space' of the internet is almost entirely controlled by a series of global private companies with too little responsibility towards children, operating significantly beyond the reach of national laws.*
>
> (GUDT, 2017, p 8)

The report favours creating an independent ombudsman to force technology companies to be more responsive to online complaints and simplify user licences to make young users understand how their data is used. GUDT (2017) research found that popular social media sites are negating their safeguarding and duty of care social responsibilities by not reporting or being regulated on how effectively they respond to young people's complaints of bullying, harassment and offensive material, citing cases of harm to children whose complaints had not been appropriately addressed. International research by the OECD (2015) found links between heavy ICT use and a range of social problems in children such as loneliness, truancy and poor attainment. The GUDT therefore argue that children should be taught digital citizenship to help them navigate the web and understand their online activity so that the internet becomes a place where *[t]hey can be citizens not just users, creative but not addictive, open yet not vulnerable to having their personal information captured and monetised by companies* (GUDT, 2017, p 3).

EDUCATION TECHNOLOGY DEVELOPMENTS

Curriculum changes

The government's advocacy of the work of American researcher E D Hirsch, as repeatedly espoused by schools minister Nick Gibb (2017), focuses on subject-based learning of a common core of facts to develop cultural literacy. These purportedly articulate the common knowledge that every citizen should have, as selected by the DfE, which should be delivered through teacher-led instruction. This approach has been criticised in terms of its potential to make education focus on rote learning of facts rather than creativity and personal development (Robinson in BBC, 2014a) and its downgrading of technical and vocational skills (Baker, 2016). In terms of digital literacy, critics argue that this knowledge focus is irrelevant in a digital era:

> *technologies will never be used in any transformative sense until we change our teaching methods... As before technology, we prioritise knowledge consumption. Once again, the grammar of schooling privileges 'knowing much' rather than encouraging faster, more efficient and socially wired connections. It will only be when we move from using technology as a newer form of knowledge consumption to seeing technology as an aid to teaching for enhanced knowledge production that there will be an effect.*

(Hattie, 2015, p 31)

Seldon concurs, strongly criticising the current curriculum's focus on knowledge over vocational and technical skills:

> *We need to focus far more, if we are to prepare our young for tomorrow's economy, and to optimise its infinite possibilities, on active as opposed to passive learning, on technical entrepreneurial skills, on personal and collaborative skills that teach us how to live intelligent and fulfilling lives, and how to work and live harmoniously with others.*

(Seldon in Baker, 2016)

Baker (2016), a former Conservative education secretary, criticises his own party's 2014 curriculum, arguing that the pace of technological change makes the subject knowledge focus inappropriate for future employment opportunities as it rapidly becomes obsolete. Baker instead argues that the required skills of the future will be technical, analytical, soft skills and business sense to interpret rather than just remember data. Arguing that the 2014 curriculum is too narrow and little different to the one introduced in 1904, he asserts that the fall in design and technology learners, due to it not being considered a core subject, needs to be reversed as it offers a combination of technical expertise, creativity and innovation that future employment needs. This criticism is echoed by the Conservative-chaired STC, which questions the traditional, subject-focused approach of its own government:

> *As digital skills are increasingly becoming essential for industrial sectors, schools will need to invest in offering high quality computer science courses and upskilling teachers so that digital skills can become more mainstream rather than as a standalone subject. The Government seems to treat computer science as a separate subject rather than a mechanism to enhance learning across other subject disciplines.*

(STC, 2016b, p 28)

Indeed, Scotland has a specific *Digital Teaching and Learning Strategy* that emphasises the importance of technology throughout the curriculum, teacher standards and training

(Scottish Government, 2016). Similarly, the radical overhaul of Welsh education emanating from their curriculum review in 2015 emphasises moving away from a subject-based focus, arguing for technology to be embedded in all subjects as with literacy and numeracy:

> *The argument for treating 'digital competence' in a similar way to literacy and numeracy has become increasingly compelling. Our children and young people already inhabit a digital world and their personal, social and educational lives are increasingly intertwined with technology in various, rapidly changing forms. Full participation in modern society and the workplace already demands increasingly high levels of digital competence and that process can only continue into a future that we cannot imagine.*

(Donaldson, 2015, p 108)

The STC (2016b), Baker (2016) and Donaldson (2015) agree that given the importance of digital skills, they should be considered as important as the current pre-eminence of maths and literacy. Baker (2016) argues that we are living in the Fourth Industrial Revolution, but that unlike previous revolutions, technological advances will shed more jobs than they create due to increasing automation and development of artificial intelligence (AI). Crucially, he argues that the rate and breadth of change across nearly all sectors means that there will be little time to retrain workers, with an estimated 15 million mainly administrative and production roles at risk within the UK (Bank of England, 2015, cited in Baker, 2016). The Royal Society concur, stating that future workers will need:

> *a mind-set that is flexible, creative and adaptive. This will be crucial to preparing today's young learners for a future economy in which the skills needed are not only unpredictable now, but will continue to change throughout their careers; a future in which workers must have the ability and confidence to continue to learn and adapt long after leaving formal education.*

(Royal Society, 2012, p 24)

Finally, considering the role of the teacher in the digital revolution, both the STC (2016b) and Baker (2016) highlight a key problem being a shortage of computer science teachers as well as the majority not holding a relevant computing qualification. The STC argue that the government needs to prioritise recruiting computer science teachers to help make delivery of computing more consistent, with many former ICT teachers lacking qualifications or confidence to teach the new subject. Although Baker argues that teaching jobs will remain, there are suggestions by some that teachers will not always be at the forefront of teaching. Professor Lucklin (STC, 2016a) argues that Intelligent Tutoring Systems will soon have a major role in delivering learning. Internationally renowned online educationalist Professor Sugata Mitra goes further, stating that: *There will be machines that can replace a good teacher, just as there will be machines that will replace a heart surgeon* (BBC, 2014b).

SUMMARY OF KEY POINTS

- Developing a computer science-based approach to the digital learning curriculum appears to be supported by a consensus of key authorities in the field.

- The renewed emphasis on computer science represents a reprise of the UK's world-leading policy to bring computers into schools in the 1980s, focusing on developing coding ability rather than rote learning of specific office/administrative-based programs.

- Ongoing teacher shortages and unmet training needs are resulting in inconsistent provision,

- Critics, including some from the current government's political party, argue that the creativity underpinning the new computing curriculum should be expanded to the English national curriculum as a whole, claiming its knowledge focus does not meet the changing employer needs caused by rapid technological innovation. Welsh curriculum reforms are attempting such an approach.

- Current government emphasis on online safety for children focuses on schools' responsibilities, but the Children's Commissioner calls for compulsory teaching of digital citizenship and more robust government action to force internet companies to meet the human rights' needs of young users.

 Check your understanding

1   What are potential limitations of technology-based learning research?

2   What reasons have been given for the current emphasis on computer coding?

3   Why is digital literacy development important for learners?

4   What are key concerns relating to learner online safety?

TAKING IT FURTHER

ATL, *IT and Data Protection Factsheets*, www.atl.org.uk/topic/technology-and-data-protection. Practical legal advice for educators from a teachers' union.

BBC, *Make it Digital*, www.bbc.co.uk/programmes/articles/4hVG2Br1W1LKCmw8nSm9WnQ/the-bbc-micro-bit. Guidance for the BBC's micro-computer for learners

CEOP, https://ceop.police.uk/safety-centre. Police child protection site for reporting online issues.

Kellsey, D and Taylor, A (2016) *The Learning Wheel: A Model of Digital Pedagogy*. Northwich: Critical Publishing. Guidance on embedding cross-curricular digital pedagogy.

Machin, L, Hindmarch, D, Murray, S and Richardson, T (2016) *A Complete Guide to the Level 5 Diploma in Education and Training*. Northwich: Critical Publishing. See Chapter 13.

Raspberry Pi, www.raspberrypi.org. Guidance for using their learner-based micro-computer.

The Tech Partnership, www.thetechpartnership.com. Employer-based network for promoting digital skills.

TED Education, www.ted.com/topics/education. Video lectures from globally renowned educationalists and technology experts.

UK Safer Internet Centre, www.saferinternet.org.uk. Organisation dedicated to promoting responsible and safe technology use for young people.

UKCCIS, www.gov.uk/government/groups/uk-council-for-child-internet-safety-ukccis. This is a group of government, industry, law academia and charity organisations dedicated to help keep children safe online.

The World Bank, *ICT and Education Policies*, www.worldbank.org/en/topic/edutech/brief/ict-education-policies. Global perspective of digital learning.

REFERENCES

Baker, K (2016) *The Digital Revolution: The Impact of the Fourth Industrial Revolution on Employment and Education*. London: The Edge Foundation. [Online]. Retrieved from: www.edge.co.uk/research/research-reports/the-digital-revolution (accessed 23 April 2017).

BBC (2014a) *The Educators: Sir Ken Robinson*. [Online]. Retrieved from: www.bbc.co.uk/programmes/b04d4nvv (accessed 23 April 2017).

BBC (2014b) *The Educators: Sugata Mitra*. [Online]. Retrieved from: www.bbc.co.uk/programmes/b04gvm7n (accessed 23 April 2017).

BBC (2015) *Computing Britain. Episode 6: Computers in Class*. [Online]. Retrieved from: www.bbc.co.uk/programmes/b06bhvsy (accessed 23 April 2017).

Brown, D (2015) *Online Safety and Inspection*. London: Ofsted. [Online]. Retrieved from: www.slideshare.net/Ofstednews/childinternetsafetysummitonlinesafetyinspection (accessed 23 April 2017).

CLA (2017) *ImagineNation: The Value of Cultural Learning.* [Online]. Retrieved from: www.culturallearningalliance.org.uk/news/new-publication-sets-out-the-value-of-arts-education (accessed 23 April 2017).

DfE (2012) *'Harmful' ICT Curriculum Set to be Dropped to Make Way for Rigorous Computer Science.* [Online]. Retrieved from: www.gov.uk/government/news/harmful-ict-curriculum-set-to-be-dropped-to-make-way-for-rigorous-computer-science (accessed 23 April 2017).

DfE (2015) *The Prevent Duty: Departmental Advice for Schools and Childcare Providers*. London: DfE. [Online]. Retrieved from: www.gov.uk/government/uploads/system/uploads/attachment_data/file/439598/prevent-duty-departmental-advice-v6.pdf (accessed 23 April 2017).

Donaldson, G (2015) *Successful Futures: Independent Review of Curriculum and Assessment Arrangements in Wales.* [Online]. Retrieved from: http://gov.wales/topics/educationandskills/schoolshome/curriculum-for-wales-curriculum-for-life/why-we-are-changing/successful-futures/?lang=en (accessed 23 April 2017).

Elwick, A, Liabo, K, Nutt, J and Simon, A (2013) *Beyond the Digital Divide*. London: CfBT. [Online]. Retrieved from: www.educationdevelopmenttrust.com/~/media/EDT/Reports/Research/2013/r-beyond-the-digital-divide-perspective-2013.pdf (accessed 23 April 2017).

Gibb, N (2017) *The Evidence in Favour of Teacher-Led Instruction*. London: DfE. [Online]. Retrieved from: www.gov.uk/government/speeches/nick-gibb-the-evidence-in-favour-of-teacher-led-instruction (accessed 23 April 2017).

Government Digital Service (2014) *Government Digital Inclusion Strategy*. [Online]. Retrieved from: www.gov.uk/government/publications/government-digital-inclusion-strategy/government-digital-inclusion-strategy (accessed 23 April 2017).

GUDT (2017) *Growing Up Digital*. Children's Commissioner. [Online]. Retrieved from: www.childrenscommissioner.gov.uk/publications/growing-digital. (accessed 23 April 2017).

Gunson, R and Thomas, R (2017) *Equipping Scotland for the Future: Key Challenges for the Scottish Skills System*. Edinburgh: IPPR Scotland. [Online]. Retrieved from: www.ippr.org/publications/equipping-scotland-for-the-future (accessed 23 April 2017).

Hattie, J (2015) *What Doesn't Work in Education: The Politics of Distraction*. London: Pearson. [Online]. Retrieved from: www.pearson.com/hattie/distractions.html (accessed 23 April 2017).

ICO (2017) *Overview of the General Data Protection Regulation (GDPR)*. [Online]. Retrieved from: https://ico.org.uk/for-organisations/data-protection-reform/overview-of-the-gdpr (accessed 23 April 2017).

IFLA (2017) *How to Spot Fake News: IFLA in the Post-Truth Society*. [Online]. Retrieved from: www.ifla.org/node/11175 (accessed 23 April 2017).

Johnson, S (2002) *Emergence: The Connected Lives of Ants, Brains, Cities and Software*. London: Penguin Books.

Meyers, E, Erickson, I and Small, R (2013) Digital Literacy and Informal Learning Environments: An Introduction. *Learning, Media and Technology*, 38(4): 355–67.

Moodle (2017) *Pedagogy.* [Online]. Retrieved from: https://docs.moodle.org/32/en/Pedagogy (accessed 23 April 2017).

Nutt, J (2010) *Professional Educators and the Evolving Role of ICT in Schools.* London: CfBT. [Online]. Retrieved from: www.educationdevelopmenttrust.com/en-GB/our-research/our-research-library/2010/r-professional-educators-and-the-evolving-role-of-ICT-in-schools-2010 (accessed 23 April 2017).

OECD (2015) *Students, Computers and Learning: Making the Connection.* [Online]. Retrieved from: www.oecd.org/publications/students-computers-and-learning-9789264239555-en.htm (accessed 23 April 2017).

Ofsted (2013) *ICT in Schools 2008–2011.* [Online]. Retrieved from: www.gov.uk/government/publications/ict-in-schools-2008-to-2011 (accessed 23 April 2017).

Ofsted (2015) *Online Safety and Inspection.* [Online]. Retrieved from: www.slideshare.net/Ofstednews/childinternetsafetysummitonlinesafetyinspection (accessed 23 April 2017).

Perry, C (2015) *Coding in Schools.* Northern Ireland Assembly. [Online]. Retrieved from: www.niassembly.gov.uk/globalassets/documents/raise/publications/2015/education/3715.pdf (accessed 23 April 2017).

Royal Society (2012) *Shut Down or Restart? The Way Forward for Computing in UK Schools.* London: The Royal Society. [Online]. Retrieved from: https://royalsociety.org/topics-policy/projects/computing-in-schools/report (accessed 23 April 2017).

Scottish Government (2016) *Enhancing Learning and Teaching through the Use of Digital Technology: A Digital Teaching and Learning Strategy for Scotland.* [Online]. Retrieved from: www.gov.scot/Resource/0050/00505855.pdf. (accessed 23 April 2017).

STC (2016a) *Robotics and Artificial Intelligence. Fifth Report of Session.* London: House of Commons. [Online]. Retrieved from: www.parliament.uk/business/committees/committees-a-z/commons-select/science-and-technology-committee (accessed 23 April 2017).

STC (2016b) *Digital Skills Crisis Second Report of Session 2016–17.* London: House of Commons. [Online]. Retrieved from: www.parliament.uk/business/committees/committees-a-z/commons-select/science-and-technology-committee (accessed 23 April 2017).

Glossary of acronyms

ACPCs	Area Child Protection Committees
AfL	Assessment for Learning
ATL	Association of Teachers and Lecturers. This union is merging with the NUT.
BBC	British Broadcasting Corporation
BERA	British Educational Research Association
CfBT	Centre for British Teachers. This changed to the Education Development Trust in 2016.
CLA	Cultural Learning Alliance
DBS	Disclosure and Barring Services
DCSF	Department for Children, Schools and Families. Now defunct, with most duties undertaken by the DfE.
DfBIS	Department for Business, Innovation and Skills. This was abolished in 2016 with responsibilities for further education transferring to the DfE.
DfE	Department for Education
DfES	Department for Education and Skills. Now defunct, with most duties undertaken by the DfE.
DPA	Data Protection Act. This will be replaced in May 2018 by the GDPR.
DSL	Designated Safeguarding Lead
EHRC	Equality and Human Rights Commission
ERA	Education Reform Act (1988)
ETF	Education and Training Foundation
FBVs	Fundamental British Values
GDPR	General Data Protection Regulation. This will replace the DPA in May 2018.
GTCE	General Teaching Council for England (abolished in 2012)
GTCNI	General Teaching Council for Northern Ireland
GTCS	General Teaching Council for Scotland
GTCW	General Teaching Council for Wales
ICO	Information Commissioners' Office
ICT	Information and Communication Technology

IPPR	Institute for Public Policy Research
ISC	Independent Schools Council
ISI	Independent School Inspectorate (ISI)
LSCB	Local Safeguarding Children's Boards
MAT	Multi-academy trust
NAHT	National Association of Head Teachers
NEET	not in education, employment and training
NET	National Education Trust
NFER	National Foundation for Educational Research
NPQH	National Professional Qualification for Headship
NPQSL	National Professional Qualification for Senior Leaders
NUT	National Union of Teachers
OECD	Organisation for Economic Cooperation and Development
OFSTED	Office for Standards in Education, Children's Services and Skills
PIAAC	Programme for the International Assessment of Adult Competencies
PIRLS	Progress in International Reading Literacy Study
PISA	Programme for International Assessment
QAA	Quality Assurance Agency
QFT	Quality First Teaching
SEND	special educational needs and disability
SIS	Schools Inspectorate Service
TALIS	Teaching and Learning International Survey
TED	Technology, Education and Design
TES	Times Educational Supplement
TIMSS	Trends in International Maths and Science Study
UCAS	Universities and Colleges Admissions Service
UKCCIS	UK Council for Child Internet Safety
UNICEF	United Nations International Children's Emergency Fund. The organisation's name changed in 1953 to the United Nations Children's Fund but it has retained its original acronym of UNICEF.

Index